MW01492229

I Thought This Was Normal

Ronald Fabian

To Jamie
from Ron
6/27/2019

Dedication

"I would like to thank my family and friends, without whom this would not have been possible. Most especially, I would like to thank Jean Lantis, who helped edit this and had more faith in me than I ever did in myself. Without her gentle kicks, this would not exist."

Table of Contents

The First Day 1

The Group Therapy Room (The Check In)................................ 8

The First Friday and Friday Night 22

Talking With Eddy... 43

Going to the Grocery Store 50

Sunday Twice Spiritual... 62

Primary Cliff... 86

First Interview of Cliff.. 97

Dr. Handle.. 102

Meeting Andy 114

A Florid Tapestry 122

Andy and the Snake 132

Games 137

Games with Faith 154

Why Are They So Mean To Him? 168

Der Romp und Schtomp... 178

Skit Night... 189

Forgiveness – It's The Law! 200

Resistance, Relapse, Denial and Death.......................... 227

Cliff Makes a Miracle 255

The First Day

My first day in treatment was really an evening, which was preceded by confusion, darkness and tears. In the early afternoon, I was taken from the hospital by a doctor to another and nearby building, which I didn't even know existed, to visit with a therapist. The doctor was not an employee of the center, but was another patient, put to do "service work," by the center. His service work was running errands, escorting new patients and being tender with them.

The therapist had already met with my sister who had told her things I would normally have disputed, because they were not quite precise enough. While in her office I took for granted that my opinion didn't count, at least not right now. The therapist had no windows in her office. She did not use her overhead lights but preferred to light the office with a desk lamp, a table lamp and a floor lamp. At that point, anything less than direct overhead yellow sunlight was darkness to me. It was like I was still at home with everything being covered in darkness.

She introduced herself to me: "Hello, my name is Sally." I stood up to shake her hand and she smiled. "We don't get a lot of that down here." I said: "What?" She said: "Men acting like gentlemen. You know, with manners." I said: "Really? This is the South. I thought everyone would be polite." She said: "Maybe in *Gone with the Wind.* Not in treatment." I smiled and sat down again. She called me by my entire first name, a mannerism she held onto throughout my stay:

"Ronald, are you ready to leave the hospital and come to treatment?" I didn't say, couldn't say, anything. How could I make a decision like that? All I could say was just that: "I can't make a decision like that. I just don't know." She said: "I mean, do you feel that you are ready to commit yourself to treatment?" I still was so confused. I started to cry. I managed to get out between sobs: "I don't know. I have no idea." She said: "Well, we think you're ready. What I mean is this: We'd like you to come and start treatment. I understand you like to cook and that you're an excellent cook. Is that right?" This is one thing I could speak objectively about. I mean, either the food tastes good or it doesn't. My food always tasted good. So I said: "Yeah, I'm a real good cook." "Great," she said. In each apartment complex, one apartment has to cook for the rest of the guys. Usually, that's between twelve and sixteen people." I felt great about that. Here was something I could do. I told her so. It looked like there was some meaning coming to me, some way to get to know the other people and to make friends. "But you can't do that all the time. Only once or twice a month. The guys you live with will push you to do more, but they will be using you. Do you understand that?" I started to cry again. For a moment, I had some minor hope of being part of a group and doing something.

Sally said: "Ronald. If you cook all the time, the other guys will be using you. If you cook all the time, you will be isolating from developing yourself and exploring why you are here. You need to create boundaries with other people. I understand you have not been good at boundaries. Is that right?" I started to cry again. That must have been information from my sister. Was it right? I thought, and then said, while trying to smile: "It's not precise, but it's right." Sally said: "Good. I understand also that you just 'came out.' Is that right?" I said: "Well, the newspapers and television stations made it hard not to. Yeah, that just happened." "Didn't anyone know you were gay: Any of your friends?" she wanted to know. I answered, quite seriously: "Well, of course the guys I went to bed with knew. And a couple of very close friends. But for the most part, I lived in a closet made out of one-way mirrors, with the mirrors facing me. I'm afraid of people here knowing." Sally said, and I didn't believe her, "This is a very gay friendly place. Some of the staff is gay." She must have noticed the look on my face. "No, I won't tell you who they are. I'm out of time, Ronald, and you need to go back to the hospital."

I stood and shook her hand. She smiled and said: "We'll being seeing you up here soon." I asked when and she said: "I don't know for sure. Today yet or tomorrow." The patient doctor came and walked me back to the hospital. It was so hot and sunny outside. We walked by pine trees down a path which was covered in these unidentifiable grayish-black strips of some material. He asked me: "Where are you from?" I told him, "Michigan." He said: "Do you know what those are?" I looked at them and said, "No." He said: "They're cut up pieces of roofing shingles. Maybe if you were from Ohio you'd have known." I said: "Not unless they were rubber." He politely chuckled. I smelled some rich, deep odor that smelled like nutmeg, like Christmas, which was so odd because it was so hot. I asked him if he knew what it was.

3

He said, in the most matter-of-fact manner: "No. But I can't really smell anymore anyway. Too much cocaine up the ol' nose."

We walked along the path until we came to a two-lane blacktop road which, I now realized, ran between the hospital and the treatment center. Across the road, and at least forty feet in the air, was a telephone line. On the center of that electronic cord, exactly in the center of the road, hung a pair of tennis shoes, as though they had been placed there on purpose. The shoe strings had been tied together but they did not overlap on the cord. It looked as though someone had just reached up and placed them there. I mentioned this to the doctor, who said: "You can't be that bad to notice those so soon. Some guys never notice them. With most, it still takes weeks. No one knows who did that. Must have been an addict though: they're hung so perfectly. Whoever did it either threw them up once or thousands of times. Addicts either only do it once, and then give up, or become incessant until they get it done." I told him: "Well, I wouldn't have done it at all." He said: "Not sober, maybe, but drunk?" I said: "Well, drinking to drunk, I would have done it all day." He said: "Yep, you're one of us."

He then said: "Did Sally tell you about the living arrangements?"

"Just that there were a bunch of guys in an apartment."

"Not exactly. They call the places we live 'domiciles.' We live in four-man apartments, two men to a bedroom. Each building has four apartments owned by the Center. Those apartments together are called 'domiciles,' or simply 'domes.' You'll hear a lot of people saying:

'Well, now in the dome....' when they want to refer what happens to where we live. The doctors here say that most of all the healing that goes on here takes place in the dome."

"So, it's sort of like college?"

He laughed. "Yeah, if you had your teachers and security guards living with you. A good part of the staff, including the directors, live here. There's a gate to get in and out. There are security guards wandering here twenty-four hours a day, seven days a week."

"It's like a minimum security prison, then?"

"Spoken like a lawyer. Probably. You can leave, really, any time you want, but the staff will know. The security guards will know. They always know. Plus a lot of the guys you live with will be spies for staff. It's sort of a prisoner or hostage mentality. If you pack up, even just to be neater than normal, someone will call it in. If you aren't eating, or if someone thinks you're using, they will let staff or security know. They think if they turn you in, then they will be treated favorably by staff."

"That sounds pretty shitty."

"Yeah, but you'll do. Everyone does. It's part of the cure." I took a sideways look at him, not sure if he was making a joke or not. He had a grin on his face that could only have come from some bitter and meaningful experience. By this time, he had walked me back to the hospital. He stood next to me as the large and locked metal doors were opened. He didn't leave me until an attendant came and walked me back to my room. My roommate was gone. I left the room and found him by the telephones. As soon as he saw me, he told the person with whom he was speaking: "I gotta go. Call ya back later." Then he said to me: "What was it like?" This was the question we constantly had for people that came from the Center to visit us or read us spiritual poems. "What is it like" was a constant refrain among the locked-down patients. It was asked by everyone. It was so constant, and so unanswerable, that it reminded me of that old Doris Day song where a kid asks her mother "What will I be?" and the mother answers: "Whatever will be will be." Those were the kinds of answers we got. Meaningless, mystical crap. I still wanted facts, but told myself I was willing to take whatever came.

I went back to the "all-purpose" room which was used at different and various times for group therapy, AA meetings, television and ping-pong. I kept looking outside the locked glass door and windows. Then I heard one of the male nurses call my name: "Fabian." I turned around and before I could say anything, he said: "Pack up your stuff. You're going up the hill." Pack my stuff? I had hardly unpacked. I also had almost nothing with me. I was ready in five minutes.

I said goodbye to my roommate, Deran. He said: "Wait a minute." He ran down the hallway just as another doctor came to take me "up the hill." This doctor was also a patient. So many of the patients were health-care professionals that the staff could just express a wish and, due to the recovered brain power of the individual patient, it was done. I found out later that some never fully recovered: especially dentists and anesthesiologists. As this doctor was grabbing my luggage, Deran came running back with a torn piece of paper in his hand: "Here.

These are the telephone numbers of the pay phones. Call me as soon as you can once you find out what goes on up there." I said "Sure," but I was so confused about where I was going.

Where I was going was back to the treatment center but into a different office. This office was run by the money people. If I had had one of those running my practice, I'd be a rich man.

The Group Therapy Room (The Check In)

The group therapy room was dark and cold. It was so cold that the staff always had sweaters in their offices which they put on as they came into the room. It somehow offended me that the sweaters never matched the outfits they wore. It took me a long time to realize the sweaters were, in the minds of the staff, strictly utilitarian, like a jail or military uniform. There were bright overhead lights, but those lights were turned off and a corner lamp was turned on. The bulb of that lamp faced the ceiling, so the light went up, then bounced back. The room itself was a square, with four white walls all of which but one was bare. On that one wall, there was a piece of manufactured, industrial art, which I am sure was picked up at the same office supply house that provided the chairs and the lamp. Even if I had been in solitary confinement for weeks in that room, I would not have become intimate with that ersatz art.

The first day I sat in that room was the Friday following my release from the detox unit of the hospital. I had no idea what to expect. The therapist smiled and sat down. She said something which I had to strain to hear. Her voice was lovely, calm, soothing, enticing, inviting and, most of all, comforting. "This is not so bad," I said to myself. I looked around the room. There were, besides the counselor, two other women. There were five other men. One was huge. Another was a domemate of mine. The counselor said: "Why don't we make a circle?"

And then everyone pulled his or her chair into a circle where it appeared that positions would not matter; But they did, just like the Round Table. Those who sat closest to Arthur got heard first. I sat right next to her right hand.

The counselor then said, in the softest, nicest voice, "I'm Kathy. Why don't we all check in? Anyone who needs time ask while you check in." I had a vague idea what she meant. We had done "check-ins" in the hospital before every group. A check-in was a quick summary of how each of us felt. And "felt" is the crucial word to addicts and alcoholics. None of us really had any idea of how we felt. That is why we abused: to either have feelings chemically induced or to run from natural feelings. Asking for time meant that you had an issue or problem you wanted to discuss.

The check-in started from the person seated closest to her left hand. It was a woman patient who looked like a grown up and seedy Barbie doll. Her hair was straw blond, held in place by glue. She had on the cowgirl Barbie outfit, tight-fitting black slacks with silver lines down the sides, which ran into black and silver cowboy boots. Her shirt matched the outfit exactly. She even had one of those skinny cloth ties on with a sliver band holding the strands together. I had noticed her in the hallway. She had stood next to the group room, giggling with the girls and smiling at the guys, just as though she were standing by her locker in the hallway of high school. As soon as she said her name, she started sobbing: "I'm Dottie. And I'll take time. Lots of it. As you all know," then she stopped talking and sobbing and looked at me and another new guy, "well you don't know, of course, you just got here. But you need to know so you can understand what I've had to put up with. My husband is the Sheriff of Renee´ Parish in Louisiana. It is the third largest parish, because you know Louisiana does not have counties, but if it did, it would be the third largest county in the state, but since we don't have counties it's called a parish, and it is the third largest, and, anyway, it produces more oil than any other single county or parish in the country. So my husband, who is the Sheriff, who is really from the backwaters of the bayou, is mad at me because I spent $5,000.00 on clothes last weekend at Neiman-Marcus and he now says he won't pay for treatment. But I had to have the clothes because, you know, I just found out he's been having an affair while I'm here and you never know, but I just might need to find another man, and why not start looking here with all the lawyers and doctor patients. Who knows? And, anyway, I never had a honeymoon. He promised me one for years but the only time he took off was to go screwing or hunting." At that Kathy said: "Dottie. We want to know how you <u>feel</u>. The history of your marriage will wait until after everyone checks in. But one thing I want to know right now is this: do you think you give all that information to avoid identifying a feeling and dealing with it?"

Dottie looked as though Kathy had slapped her. There was some history here too. "Kathy, you are always telling me how to speak and what I should say, and you say these are not my feelings, but they are." Kathy said: "Dottie, feelings are very basic. They are not about the justification of spending money at a store that most people have never been in let alone are able to afford. They are simple: are you mad, sad, glad or afraid?"

Dottie said: "You just don't understand. While I'm here trying to get better, he went out on me. I can't compete with some woman, probably some convict, I can't see."

Kathy, using a more firm voice said, "Mad, sad, glad or afraid?" Dottie started to speak and Kathy interrupted her saying: "Mad, sad, glad or afraid?" Dottie then said: "Well, can I have more than one feeling?" Kathy said: "Don't ask me. Tell me." "Well," Dottie said. She always said "well" before she spoke about meaningful things, as though she had to slow down and process whether what she was about to say was meaningful or not. "Well," she said, "I'm mad, sad and afraid. I'm mad because he went out on me after he promised not to, especially with our daughter's wedding coming up, and I don't even know if I can go to that because you haven't given me permission yet to leave and...." Kathy again interrupted her, but this time with a look. "Okay," Dottie said, "I'm sad because I'm here, and I can't hold his attention from here, and I'm afraid he'll want to divorce me once he finds out that younger women will go out with him." Kathy said so soothingly but with a lash: "You know, if you had just said that to begin with, all of us could have helped you instead of listening to you dance around the problem. Let's finish our check-ins, see who else needs time and how much time we have left before we get back to you. Help yourself and try to pay attention to the others."

Next to Dottie sat a skinny black, middle-aged guy. His clothes looked as though he had just stepped out of a Brooks Brother catalog. They were picture perfect. He said: "I'm Lee. I'm an alcoholic. Or I guess I am. At least, that's what I've been told. Anyway, I feel just fine today. I've been here about two weeks and I'm beginning to get it. That's it. I'll pass."

Kathy said: "Oh, really? That's good. You were ready to leave yesterday. Can you tell us what happened between then and now?"

"Well," Lee said, "Yesterday I was all worried about my wife and kids and my business. But last night I spoke with my partner, my wife, my accountant, my lawyer and my brother...." At this, Kathy looked very intently at Lee. "I know, I know," he said, "I'm only supposed to be on the telephone fifteen minutes a day. But this was important." Kathy looked at him from the top of her eyes and quietly said: "Your recovery is important too. Why do you spend so much time on the telephone instead of on recovery?" "I don't spend that much time on the telephone." Kathy responded: "Really? That's not what I've been told in staffing." I didn't know what she was talking about: staffing. But apparently Lee did. He looked shocked and then he looked resigned. He said: "You guys do time our calls, don't you? Do you listen in, too?" "Lee," she said, "assume that we don't time them, but that one of your roommates complained for the tenth time that you were on the phone so much no one else could use it. Or assume that we do time them. Whatever you want to believe is okay. But you know that it is a rule violation to stay on the telephone as much as you do. Anything that really needs to be said can be said in fifteen minutes. When you stay on the phone as much as you do, you avoid treatment. You stay where you were. Your mind is on the other end of the line and not with us. It's also old behavior for you to get on the phone and bark orders."

Wow! What a lot of thoughts! "Avoid treatment...timing phone calls....old behavior." Lee then said: "Kathy, I wonder if you treat the white executives here the same way." Kathy sighed: literally. "Lee, you're an addict. Skin color doesn't matter. Crack cocaine doesn't matter. White people beat their wives and children and so do blacks. The race issue is another way of avoiding treatment."

"You wouldn't say that if you were black."

"Well, I'm not. But I do say it. Let's move on and then come back."

The next guy was a dentist. "I'm Chad. I'm just fine today." Kathy smiled sweetly and said: "Bob, remember that fine is not a feeling or emotion. It's a knit." "Huh?" he said. "A knit." She and the women giggled "Fine," she said, "refers to a weave of cloth, or the weather, or the grade of flour. Chad, you certainly must be feeling something other than 'fine.'" Chad looked totally confused. You could tell that he didn't know whether to smile or frown. He actually acted like a goofy eight grader. He bent down in his chair, lowered his head, and then looked up like he was a puppy waiting for a treat, trying to be charming. A dentist trying to be charming is an impossible concept or reality, which is why he, who could have been Richard Nixon's facial twin with heavy jowls, sweat, beard, and feral smile, looked goofy. There is no other word. "Well," he said, "I guess I'm worried." Kathy smiled her patented soft smile, with her liquid eyes and gentle smile saying "trust, comfort, love," and spoke: "What are you worried about?" "My wife. My kids. My wife is sick. This is the second rehab I've been in during the last five years. I'm not rich. But I can't work until you guys give the okay. My license to prescribe has been temporarily suspended."

Kathy said: "I'm not sure, but, I wonder...." and paused. I found out later to watch out when she said: "I'm not sure, but..." or just smiled and then paused. Both behaviors were, I later discovered, tricks to get us to open up. The smile, the eyes, the face, the expressions all looked comforting and soft but they were the thin, nearly invisible edges of the opener to slice our tight and thick skins of protection and to let out the poison. "I wonder," she repeated, "if I wouldn't react in the same way if I were in the same situation. That is a lot to be worried about. I can't talk for you, of course, but I'd be scared if all that was going on with me. Do you think that maybe, just maybe, you have a little fear going on? Maybe fear that you don't want to touch or talk about?" Chad's attempt at cuteness stopped. His puppy face, waiting for a treat, disappeared and he looked like he was about ready to go into rigor mortis. "Uh," he said, "uh, well, I, um." He couldn't form words. He had more consonant sound explosions than a frog farting. That's all I could think of, too, though I must admit I've never actually seen the event, but that's what his face reminded me of. Kathy kept her face immobile yet liquid. "Uh, well, um," he said, "well, my dad used to be sort of rough with me once in a while and, well...." At this point his eyes started to move as though some fast bright thing was going back and forth in front of him. "But, he taught me to win, and I used to play football even though I'm a small guy, and I won, and I'm going to lick this too!" No one moved or said anything. It felt like something more should be coming out, like there should be some description of what his father did or explanation of what winning was, but he said nothing. His facial expression was new. It was the look of the eight-grade ass kisser who's violent in the halls and locker rooms to those less aggressive yet smarmy around those in authority. Anyway, Kathy said: "Maybe tomorrow you can identify some more feelings and we can talk about them." Chad said: "Oh, yes! I'll do that tonight! I'll think about that and get a list...." Kathy interrupted: "No, don't think. Feel. And if you really feel, you won't need a list."

It's hard not to think in clichés, but I was more than a little confused myself. Now I was glad that my placement in the circle was last for the sole reason that there was a chance we'd run out of time before it was my turn. I started staring at the ceiling.

Next was Vivian, a professor of physics at some small, prestigious East Coast college that only those worried about titles and position had ever heard of. She said: "I know how I feel. I feel worried. I wonder if I should be mad, but worried is like being afraid so I know that's okay." Kathy smiled her number fourteen smile of welcome and comfort. "Vivian. That's a lovely name. But you don't need our approval for your feelings. What's important is for you to identify how you feel. Fear is a feeling. Can you tell us what you're afraid of?" Vivian obviously didn't expect a follow-up question. Her face gave her away. What was this? A news conference? Why don't you submit your questions in writing 24 hours in advance. But she was game. "Well, I'm afraid to live without alcohol. I'm afraid to live by myself. And I'm afraid to go home." Kathy's smile had now turned in that liquid mercury way to one of support, solidarity, empathy and concern. How she got so much out of a smile was amazing. Though I was really interested in what Vivian was going to say, I couldn't stop thinking about that smile. Amazing. Was there a class in college that taught you that? Then she said: "Why are you afraid to go home?" "Well, my husband likes to beat me when I sleep." There was an audible intake of breath from the others in the room. The room, which had been very cold, seemed like a funeral parlor now. You know the feeling: dim lights, cool, distant and don't touch! It might be catching! But it was so interesting in a very clearly defined morbid way. Luckily for us blood-suckers, therapy itself demanded more attention. Kathy's smile turned into a real face, one which maybe had not heard this one before. She showed us how smart she really was by asking the only truly intelligent question: "What do you mean, he beats you in your sleep?" "He and I get drunk every night. He used to beat me when I was awake, but then I stayed in the basement until he went to sleep or passed out. Then I would go to bed." I couldn't help it. I had to interrupt: "With him?" She looked at me in shock. "Of course with him. Do you think I'd sleep with someone else?" I didn't say anything, but it took all I had at that moment not to. "I had to sleep with him. He was my husband. After a while, I was drinking so much that I'd pass out too, but he'd wake me up by beating me. I took pills then, too, on top of the alcohol to sleep through it, but even if I did I'd wake up with bruises I couldn't explain. I didn't like that. I liked to know how I got them." I couldn't hold back: "Why not sleep in a different room so that you didn't have to worry about bruises at all?" She said, as though I were an idiot ant and she was explaining the chemicals in "Raid" just before she hit the spray button, "I already told you. He is my husband."

"Hi. I'm Tom," said the next person, a guy who looked about 35 or 40. He was healthy looking, well built, compact. He had black, short hair, round John Lennon glasses, and a big grin. It was almost a smile and he showed some teeth, otherwise it would have been a smirk. What was going on with me that I noticed so intently what people's faces were doing? "I feel a little anxious today. I get to go home this weekend and see my wife and kids. I feel a little happy today too. I'll pass." Kathy said nothing. She just looked at him. He changed his smirk/grin into a smile. She smiled too. He really smiled then, with a great, engaging and infectious smile. Kathy smiled too, but hers was somewhat a smile of doubt and inquiry. If that sounds unrealistic, it seemed that way to me too, but I had never seen a smile like hers and that is the only way I can describe it. It wasn't quite an "Oh, yeah?" smile but it was challenging. Tom kept looking at her. He crossed his legs, sat up on one side of his ass, leaned forward and said: "What?" Kathy said nothing but raised her eyebrows a little and furrowed her brow. "What?" he said again. "C'mon, Kathy. What?"

"Have you made sleeping arrangements with your wife?" Tom

blushed and re-crossed his legs, sitting up on the other side of his ass. "We're going to talk about it." Kathy said: "That's something you might want to get arranged ahead of time. Not knowing where you are sleeping for sure can lead to a lot of tension. Your expectations and hers can clash." Sleep? He's going home. He'll sleep in his house, won't he? Oh, boy, I must still be drugged from the detox. She's talking about fucking, not sleeping! I am an idiot.

"No, Kathy. I've told her I'll sleep wherever she wants me to. She just has to tell me." "Tom, you didn't ask for time, but I think we need to finish the check-ins and come back to you, since you're going home for the weekend." "Oh, Kathy." It came out like a moan. He had been through this before and did not like it.

Next was a guy I immediately dubbed "The Sweater" when I had seen him first sit down in the room. The name wasn't because of what he wore, but because his face was so wet it looked like someone had just thrown water on him. He was huge; At least six and a half feet and probably 280 pounds. He had crooked teeth and lips that looked like slits. His eyes were tiny, round, rough holes about the size and shape of the holes on the side of milk cartons made by pencils. He was scary. "Ummm," he said. "I'm Dan. I'm scared. That's all I can say." I expected Kathy to smile and say something to him. Instead, she frowned. "Scared?" she said, as she hunched down as small as she could go. "Why would we scare you?" She was acting like a frightened child. I couldn't figure it out. This guy was scary so why would she act scared? Why wouldn't she sit up straight, and tall, and get into his shit? "After all," she said, "look at you. You're a big man. You're more than big. I bet no one picks on you! I bet you could pick me up with one hand and knock out poor Tom there with the other." Tom screwed up his face to make a "Who? Me?" look. Dan dropped his jaw and we could see his tiny uneven teeth. "Well, maybe now. Not that I would do or even think of doing anything like that. But not growing up. I didn't get big until my last year of high school. And I had a horrible stutter. When I get nervous I still stutter." Kathy smiled and said: "You're not stuttering now. Maybe you're not so scared." "No," he said, "I am scared." Kathy said, in a perfect Southern Belle voice: "Of little ole' me?" Dan stopped talking and quite obviously thought of a response. "No, I'm not scared of you. I'm scared of the situation. I hear all these terrible rumors about staff, and licensing, and what it costs, and going back to work, and how marriages break up...." Kathy sat up straight, leaned forward and said, as though she were the chair of an executive board: "You have given yourself a lot to be scared of. Are you sure you don't want to add to that list? That would keep you here a long time. Then you wouldn't have to worry about going back to work or home, would you?" Something clicked in me. It must have in Dan, too. "No, you don't understand. I love my wife. She is my soul mate. I want to go home. I want to return to work." Kathy said: "Hmmm. Well, you just got here. Let's not worry about all that today, shall we. Let's move on."

There was one more person and then me. This was a very attractive woman in her late thirties. Dark short hair, light eyes and in good shape. She looked like one of those women who rode horses. As

19

soon as she spoke, I discovered she was from the genteel South. "Hi. I'm Bonnie. I just got here, but I was here before and had moved into three-quarters." I got this unknowing look on my face. She noticed it, laughed and said: "Three quarters is where you go to live after you've finished treatment if staff thinks, or if you think, you need some more structured time before you return to the 'real world.'" She looked at Kathy and said: "Yes, Kathy, I know this is the real world. I know that no matter where I am it is the real world because that is where I am. Still, in the 'other world' we're not surrounded by therapists or rules. Anyway, I got caught drinking and have been removed from three-quarters and put back on the Hill until staff figures out what to do with me. How am I feeling? I don't know."

Kathy said: "Bonnie, staff would do a better job if you'd tell us why you started drinking again, and why." "Kathy," Bonnie said, "I don't know." Kathy said pleadingly: "Let's take some time on it, okay?" Bonnie said: "Sure. I'd like to know, too."

Next was my turn. "Hi. I'm Ron. This is my first group here. I'm a little nervous. I'm also real cold." That got a laugh. It's funny the stupid things you will laugh at when tense. Kathy looked at me with a serious face and no smiles. She said: "Why do you have to make a joke?" I froze. I felt as though she had slapped me. I couldn't think of a good one-liner so I was honest. "I just thought that with all the painful things people have talked about that it was time for a laugh." She said: "You're not in front of a jury. You're not here to entertain. Why don't you think these people have the right to be sad, or mad, or afraid? Do you think being glad is the only acceptable emotion?" I was paralyzed. I couldn't say anything. I was so close to her that I could touch her without reaching. I wanted to be on the other side of the room, on the other side of the door. The hospital looked good to me right then. I even started thinking that maybe jail was better. I didn't have to feel there, and in the hospital I was drugged up by licensed professionals. Now, I was on my own. "No," I said. "It's okay to feel bad. I guess." Kathy said: "Haven't you really spent most of your life running from feeling sad? Do you think it would be beneficial to learn how to feel sad and then let it go instead of hanging on to it?" I said: "I don't hang on to my bad feelings." She said: "Really. I thought they might define you at some basic level. Let's go to those who asked for time and for tomorrow I want you to think when it's okay for you to feel sad."

The First Friday and Friday Night

On Friday, my case manager stopped me in the hallway just before I was ready to go back to the apartment and gave me a thirty-page questionnaire. Her name was Traci and she was probably about 30 years old and very thin. Even though it was very hot outside, she wore a long dress and a sweater. She stopped me in a corner by the therapists' offices, a location which I hated. I felt uncomfortable and not quite trapped. The area was still so new to me and I had not figured out where boundaries and territories were. People walked by us with obvious individual purposes. The hallway was not wide enough for she and I to have any privacy. I started having an out-of-body feeling, as though I were not part of the scene but was instead observing it, floating in the air just above and behind my head. As she handed me the questionnaire, she said: "Answer it as soon as you can, but don't rush. Be honest and complete. It is totally confidential. No one else will see it."

As I floated, I was looking at myself looking at the two of us. I had this inordinate desire to please her. Even though answering written questions was something with which I was extremely familiar, I was worried about failing the form and displeasing her. I wanted to please her so badly. I was still floating in the hallway and could see that I had a distressed look on my face. She kept saying: "Don't worry." She laughed and then said: "Ron! Breathe!" I had not noticed that I was not breathing. Traci then said: "Everyone has to fill one of these out. It is to educate us about you. It's not complicated but it is long, and it asks very personal and intimate questions. Just answer the questions honestly."

She had acted so nicely that I began to feel a little more comfortable. I rejoined my body and said: "I'll do it tonight." She got a serious and calming look upon her face. "Ron," she said, "tomorrow is Saturday. You won't be here. You will be in "Real People." Anyway, even if you were here, I won't be here. Just get it done in the next week." With that she smiled and left, saying "Don't forget you're on 'Buddy.'" This was the name of the rule which forbad new patients to be alone except when in the rehab building itself.

I looked at the form and put it in my notebook. People were still walking in the hallway with definite purpose, but there was one guy in his mid-thirties with a tie and a Hitler-youth moustache standing still. He was looking very stern at another guy who was wearing a T-shirt and shorts. Mr. Moustache was talking to the T-shirt. I couldn't hear much, but I did hear him say in a disgusted tone of voice: "C'mon, Brand, you expect me to believe that? It's not like you just got here...." And then I could hear nothing, but from the look on Brand's face I bet he wished he could separate from himself like I did. I assumed Mr. Moustache was staff and Brand was a patient because of the clothes and the attitude differences.

There was no way to get around them without bumping into one or the other, so I walked up to Mr. Moustache and said: "Excuse me." You could tell that strangers bumping into him was nothing new. He

23

moved so I could just get by him with our shoulders touching and continued talking to the Brand guy: "It's not like you haven't been to rehab before. It's not like you're a virgin to all this. You know the routine. How stupid do you think I am..." Mr. Moustache sure didn't take any shit.

I walked out the back door of the building to the only area people were allowed to smoke, looking for one or another of my domemates to walk back to the apartments with me. It was incredibly hot and humid, the kind of weather in which you uncontrollably sweated by just being in it. There was a concrete patio with cheap plastic chairs and tables. Beyond the patio was a field of scrub grass which was yellow, brown and green. Surrounding the grass area were tall and very scraggly pine trees. There was a strong fetid odor of decaying vegetation, almost a sour garbage smell, mixed with the sickening fumes of cigarette smoke.

I saw my roommate, Eddy, who waved at me with a lit cigarette in his hand. He came over and asked: "How you doing?" I said, "Okay, I think. I just got this huge form to fill out." He said: "Yeah, the psycho-sociological sexual just-how-weird-are-you-weirdo questionnaire. I hear the staff reads those on Monday mornings in staffing conference and laughs till their sides hurt so much they snort their coffee out their noses." I must have looked panicked because he said: "Relax. Just kidding, man. Are you done for the day?" I said, "Yeah, I think so, except for answering this." He said: "You know you can't go back to the apartment alone?" "Yeah," I said, "Can you go back with me?" "No, I think some of us are going to go downtown. Hang out here for a while, and I'll find someone to go with you." I was disappointed that he didn't ask me to go with him but was glad enough that he was trying to help me by finding someone

He went in the building, still smoking, which was against the rules. Less than a minute later he came out with Brand, the guy Mr. Moustache had been lecturing. Eddy said: "Ron, have you met Brand?" I said: "No, but I've seen him as part of a lecture." Brand screwed up his face as though he didn't understand what I meant, so I said: "I saw that guy with the moustache sort of yelling at you in the hallway." Brand smiled a huge used-car salesman grin and said in a slow, southern dumb boy voice with all the who-me-worried disdain he could assemble: "Who, him? Ah, that's nothing. He said he caught me in 'another lie' so he had to yell at me. That's what he gets paid for. He's my primary." Eddy said: "Brand, you know you lie all the time." Brand said, "Ah, Eddy. C'mon man, who's the real drunk here?" Eddy said: "Brand, I know I'm a drunk. I'm not a liar about it. You're a drunk, an addict, a near suicide, a thief, a pervert and a liar." I said nothing. I had no idea what to say. But I was fearful that they would get into an argument, so I said: "Primary?" "Yeah," Brand said. "My main therapist. He's the best here. Who's yours?" I said: "I don't know. I've got Kathy for something. Maybe it's her." Brand said: "Let me see your notebook," which he grabbed out of my hand and opened. He pointed to the inside and said: "All your therapists are listed on the inside. See, Kathy is your process group, and the guy you call Mr. Moustache is your primary. His

25

real name is James, but we all call him 'Cliff' because he thinks he can cut you open. He thinks he's so tough." Eddy said: "Brand, he does cut you open, and he is tough. You piss your pants every time you see him. Listen. Take Ron back to the apartments, but wait for the other new guys too." Brand said: "You're not senior addict. You can't tell me what to do." Eddy said: "Brand, give yourself a break and be nice. Cliff might hear about it and give you a break." Brand's face looked as if he were actually calculating being considerate to me and the other new guys. He was so obvious. "Yeah, sure. Okay. I'll take care of them." "And don't leave them alone," Eddy said as he walked away.

Brand looked at me and gave me this goofy smile which he must have thought was charming. He spoke to me as if I were a non-English-speaking foreigner: slowly and loudly, as though the cadence and volume could get through when knowledge couldn't. "You wait right here and don't move. I'm going to go into the building and find the other new guys."

I said, pointing at the rehab building, which was not only the only building near, it was the only one we could see, "you mean that building there?" Brand looked at me, apparently not knowing if I were serious or not. "Yeah, that one." "Okay," I said. "And I promise that I won't move. Can I blink my eyes?" Brand must have started to figure out that I was some kind of Northern smart-ass, but he said nothing. Maybe he had heard that I lived in Detroit when I was in law school. "I'll be right back."

As soon as he left, I took out the questionnaire and started reading it. Simple, standard stuff on the first page. Name, age, date of birth, home address, office address, occupation, and years of education. The next page was family background. Parents and siblings. Alive or dead. Cause of death. Then there were little boxes next to phrases, please mark the box yes or no: Emotional abuse: ☐yes ☐no; Physical abuse: ☐yes ☐no; Sexual abuse: ☐yes ☐no. I stopped breathing. No one was around, so I didn't start to fly out of my body. I turned the page. "Give your history of spirituality;" Then an entire lined page upon which to write the history. Might as well start with the easy ones. I pulled out a pen, drew a diagonal line across the page from the bottom-left corner to the top-right corner, and then across the line, I printed in firm and large letters: "I hate priests!"

Brand came out with two guys next to him. Both were doctors. One was Billy, a rich kid who went to medical school on his dad's money and who barely practiced due to his drug addiction, and the other was Michael, a poor kid who went to medical school on loans which he was still paying, and which were in default because he paid his dealer first. Both were short, in their early thirties, but Billy had stayed in shape while Michael had already developed a gut beyond control. He wore cheap T-shirts and shorts. Neither the shirt nor the shorts could contain or properly get around the gut. The bottoms of his shorts were so tight they cut into his skin. Billy had a look of deep sadness on his face. He was staring at the ground while he shuffled alongside Brand and Michael. Michael was smiling, and, by comparison, seemed like he was vibrating. The difference may have been due to the fact that Billy was a champion pill popper of downers, taking, on some days, hundreds of "mother's little helpers" while Michael was a huge fan of cocaine and nitrous oxide. He was a champion of laughing gas, telling us it was like being high on LSD, with visions, music and everything, all of which ended just as soon as the gas did. "No flashbacks!" he said as though that were some sort of victory.

Brand smiled again and said: "let's go y'all," and we dutifully followed him. "Now, I've been here four months, so I think I should tell you some of the more important rules." He led us back into the building. "First, you're not supposed to cut through the building to get to the path back to the apartments." We followed him in the hallway around the therapists' offices, into the lobby and out the front door. "You're never supposed to go in or out the front door except for the day you get here and the day you leave. I guess the directors don't want to see addicts and alcoholics any more then they gotta. And never go in or out the staff door. They get real upset about that." "Why?" Michael asked. "That seems silly, especially considering the money we're all paying for this." Brand answered: "They're just trying to make us follow rules. Seems like they think none of us are rule followers. Oh, they'll catch you on those rules, and they won't let you out 'til they think you follow them just right." Michael said: "So, what's the big deal? We follow them, then, right?" "Oh, man," Brand said. "Don't you know anything? They have a saying: 'Compliance is defiance.'"

I was totally confused. First he was telling us that following rules was so important that you didn't get out until you followed them just right, but he was openly breaking them. Then his saying told us that actual compliance was actually rule breaking. Billy said: "So how are we supposed to know which ones to follow?" Brand said: "I dunno. Just don't get caught." Michael said: "Well, maybe when our brains start to work again, we'll figure it out." I said: "It's sort of Buddhist. You know, 'all truth lies in paradox.' I don't know which is what yet, but there is a sense of rightness about it." Brand said with some anger: "I don't know what the fuck you're talking about, man." Michael gave a small laugh and said with some glee: "Hey, man, he's a lawyer! And I bet he's got another degree in religion." "No," I said, "philosophy." Michael yelped and said: "Even worse! A lawyer with a degree in philosophy. Boy, are we going to have some interesting talks."

Brand was apparently upset that attention had been taken from him. His face started to turn white and his jaws were clenched. "Well, with all your education you're still here." I didn't say anything but thought "Jesus! I am tired of managing difficult personalities. And I've got to live with this guy!" Michael said: "Somehow, I don't think education has anything to do with addiction."

We walked in silence for a while. We were on the dirt path between the rehab center and the hospital. Both sides of the path were thick with trees, flowers and scrub growth. The very strong smell of decay surrounded us, but then the smell of something overpowering cut through it all. I tried to figure it out but couldn't. The smell reminded me of Christmas. Then I figured it out: nutmeg. But did nutmeg grow in scrub growth on the outskirts of a huge city? I didn't know, and I sure didn't want to challenge Brand's knowledge so I kept the odor to myself. No one else said anything, but it gave me comfort. Christmas was always a very special time for me and my family. It was the one certain time of the year that I knew I belonged somewhere, which was at my brother-in-law and sister's house, but that had ended with his death two years ago.

We walked by the hospital. Brand said: "How long were you guys in detox?" Billy said: "I detoxed back home and flew straight here." Michael said: "Oh, at least ten days. It's hard for me to remember. I was pretty fucked up when I got here." Brand looked at me and said: "How about you, Mr. Philosopher?" I thought: "Oh, no, already this guy's got it in for me." Then I said: "I'm not sure either. I think three days. Yes. I got here on Tuesday and came up on the hill on Thursday. So, depending on how you want to count, three days and two nights. Sort of like a cruise you'd win." Brand gave me a nasty look, but both Michael and Billy laughed. Billy started to smile and sang: "A three-hour tour," obviously referring to "Gilligan's Island." Even Brand laughed at that.

We walked past the hospital to a truly wooded area. Brand said: "Now, you're not allowed to walk this path alone 'till you're off 'Buddy.' Never walk it at dark and try not to walk it alone. They found a body here a couple of years ago." Billy said: "Is that an urban legend or for real?" Brand apparently didn't know what an 'urban legend' was, but he picked up on the "for real" part of the sentence. "For real, man," he said, like we were idiots. "This is Atlanta and we live in a real rough neighborhood." The path actually made me feel like I was at home. I live in the woods and am surrounded by nature. Brand said: "There's white tailed deer here but don't kill one, man." Billy was really waking up now: "With what? Our hands? For some unknown reason, they took our scalpels and guns from us when we checked in. I suppose Ron could talk it to death, but lawyers charge for that."

We had reached the back side of the apartments. It was the only area without a gate or fences topped with barbed wire. Michael said: "We could walk out of here anytime, couldn't we?" Brand looked at him like he was crazy and said: "Why would you wanna do that, man?" Michael said: "Oh, I don't know. To get drugs maybe; Or to get laid; Or to just get out of here." Brand had a you-stupid-shit look on his face saying, "You'd be crazy to leave here." Billy and I looked at each other, and before I could say it, Billy did: "You have to be crazy to get in here!" and the three of us laughed. Brand looked at his shoes and said: "I don't know about you guys." Michael said: "Hey, lighten up, 'man,' it's only a three-hour tour!" I began to realize I was not the only one who realized that Brand begged management.

When we got to our apartment building Brand told us: "You're not allowed to be in your apartments unless somebody off 'Buddy' is in there with you." I didn't know this, but Michael and Brand were roommates so Michael was covered, but there was no one in my apartment or Billy's. Billy said: "So if we can't be in our apartment, what rule says we can't sit outside together in the breezeway?" Brand said: "I don't know. But I'm sure there is a rule." Billy said: "We'll chance it," so he and I sat together while he lit a cigarette. "Want one?" he asked? "No, thanks. I quit twelve years ago and that's one addiction I don't want to revisit. How long have you smoked?" "Let's see," he said, "I got here yesterday, so about 24 hours." "Are you kidding?" I asked. "Nope. I've got to have something." He said this with anger, as though he were owed something which he had been denied.

We sat there in the shade of the apartment building overhang in stifling heat and humidity. Billy looked down at the concrete walkway. His face was half hidden but I could see that his earlier look of sadness had returned. Normally I would have asked him what was wrong. Now, though, I said nothing and just sat there. He said: "Do you have any kids?" I simply said: "No." For a minute neither of us said anything. A minute of silence is a long time, especially with a stranger. Then he said: "You know, I've lost my license. I don't know how I'm going to support my wife and kids." I said: "This is one of those lucky times for someone like me, then. I only have my dogs and myself." I had a professionally taken photo of my dogs in my wallet. I took it out and handed it to him, laughing, "Most people show pictures of their kids. These are my dogs. Tuck is the larger one. He's the male. Dora is the smaller one with the curly hair. I call her Dora because she's adorable. They are brother and sister." I started to cry. I felt embarrassed, ashamed and overwhelmed. Billy looked up at me and said with sincerity I at first didn't believe. "It's okay, man, I cry when I think of home, too." And then he started to get tears in his eyes. I said: "I had made plans to kill myself. The only thing which had been keeping me alive were my dogs, and their love for me. I had disassociated with everyone else including one of my sisters with whom I am very close. She's the reason I'm here. Once I got arrested, she arranged this whole thing. I'm still in a fog about it." I kept crying and then Billy pulled out a photo from his wallet. It was a dress-up picture of him, his wife and their six children. "Six kids!" I said. "Oh my God! I didn't know people still had families that large." As I looked closer at the photo I said: "Are you sure this is your wife? She looks great." Billy smiled and said: "Yeah, that's Cheryl. She's fantastic." We both wiped our eyes on our arms and sniffled a little. "But I'm not sure she's going to put up with this. I'm not there to help her. Our nanny quit because Cheryl found out she was using with me and this is my second time in rehab. If I don't make it, I don't know what's going to happen."

"When I was in jail," I said, "I was held in a glass suicide prevention cell for three days. One of my attorney friends visited me. She has epilepsy and had just gotten her prescription refilled. I wrestled her for her purse and tried to take all her pills, whatever they were." Billy interjected, "Probably Phenobarbital." "I wanted to die so bad then." Billy looked directly at me, but he had a different look on his face: one of professional competence. "Well," he said, "They might not have killed you, but they sure wouldn't have done you any good. Besides, you would have been taken to the hospital and had your stomach pumped. Then that suicide cell might have looked good." I thought for a moment and said: "I don't know. I was there for three days. They offered me a private shower, but I could hardly move. The guards were all very nice and considerate, but all I did was cry. I couldn't eat. There was a bare 100-watt light bulb always on in the cell and I couldn't sleep. When I was finally scheduled to go to court, a friend brought in some clean clothes from home. It seemed like the life I had before I was in jail was so far away. It seemed like it was a fantasy, an illusion, a dream and a nightmare. I touched those clothes as though they were a gift from God. All I could think of was how great my life could have been, but how miserable I was. I just wanted to die. I prayed to God to let me die. In a way, He did. The old life is gone forever and now I'm going to have some kind of new life. I don't know what it's going to be and it's scary, but my old life was miserable."

Billy said: "Well, I don't normally play one-upmanship, but when I said I detoxed at home, I should have told you the whole truth. I did, but I was in a locked, suicide prevention cell in the hospital where I had been chief of surgery. Now, that's a world turned upside down. What were you arrested for?" Yes, indeed, what was I arrested for. "I'm not going to hide it, just let me say, for now, for being drunk and stupid. I'll tell you later, but I'm not up for it right now. Besides, I've got this questionnaire to fill out." The retreat of paperwork, of "duty" kept me from telling him what I wanted to say. I had been arrested for letting young adult men come to my house to party and then trying to have sex with them. My sister had taken me to a psychiatrist the Sunday before I came to treatment. He asked me: "When was the last time you had sex without being drunk?" That question knocked me off of whatever fragile perch I was on after being released from jail. Sobbing, I told him, "I can't remember when." He said to me: "Listen. I've come into my office on a Sunday and taken time away from my family. I used to be just like you. I thought alcohol, drugs and sex was love. This is going to sound cold, but if you don't get honest with yourself and those around you, you'll be dead in four months."

I wanted to tell Billy that, but I was afraid of being judged and disliked. I started to say something, but then the Professor came up the walk loudly singing some Salsa song. I couldn't understand a word or even in what language it was. "Hey," he said, "sad faces here! Don't worry. It can only get better." I sang to him: "It can't get no worse." He looked at me quizzically. Billy looked at me knowingly. I said: "'It's Getting Better' Sgt. Pepper. The Beatles. Paul sings: 'I've got to admit it's getting better' and John sings: 'It can't get no worse.'" The Professor said, "Ah, yes, of course, as a white North American of your age, the Beatles most probably constitute your entire intellectual storehouse." I laughed and said, "Well, a lot anyway."

The Professor said: "Tonight is Friday. It is the night we all see a movie and go out to eat. We are only supposed to eat out once a week, which is usually on Saturday. But the movie houses here sell hot dogs which, if you eat, is a meal. Now, I think hot dogs should be illegal, but most others don't agree with me. So those of us who don't like to eat hot dogs in the theater instead eat something outside of the theater and then go to a movie." I said, "Well, I don't know. I don't want to get into trouble or anything. This Brand guy seems big on following the rules when others are looking." The Professor said: "Oh, you have met

Brand? Yes, a fine and totally insane self-server. Be careful of him. I do not think the two of you will like each other. You may be too honest and he is not honest enough. No. Not even close. We will make sure you are with me tonight. Normally, Eddy, Paul and I go to eat and then to the movies. You will be part of us. In any event, you must appreciate the hot dog argument. It is worthy of a Jesuit, eh?"

"So, why are you two sitting outside on this miserable day?" the Professor asked. Billy said: "Brand said we couldn't be alone in the apartments because we are both on 'Buddy,' but that he didn't know of a specific rule which said we couldn't sit together outside." "Ah," the Professor said, "I am not the only one who appreciates Jesuit logic, eh? You have created your own 'rule around the rule' without even knowing it. This is a sign. You are true addicts. But, see, and Brand should have told you this, the unofficial Rule-Around-the-Rule for your situation is to simply go into your apartments and keep all the doors open. You are not really then alone." I asked, "Are you sure?" He said, "But, yes, of course. And anyway, only Brand would tell on you, and he is most assuredly now taking one of his very long and selfish afternoon naps. No, do not ask me more. He will confess them to you nightly. Go into your apartments and sleep or feel miserable, but certainly make sure the air conditioning is on so that at least you can feel cool."

"Well," I said, "I've got this form to fill out." "Oh, yes," said the Professor, "You are so very eager. Well, go do it and I will collect you for the movie and for dinner."

I went into the apartment, keeping the door open, and went into my bedroom, also keeping that door open. It was so dark in the bedroom that I turned on the lamp next to my bed. I sat on my bed and took the questionnaire from my notebook. I went back to the squares ☐ Yes ☐ No and started marking all of them yes. It didn't take too long to finish it. I must have laid back because it took Eddy grabbing my arm and saying: "Hey, wake up! Ron. It's time to eat and see a movie." I must have looked blank because he said: "This is our chance to pretend we're normal." I said, "Uh, okay," but I was worried that he may have seen my questionnaire. I had no secrets, really, anymore and those I had I didn't want, but I wanted to be the person who told my story, though it probably didn't matter. He walked into the bathroom. "I'll be right out. Don't fall back asleep." I said: "I'm not going to fall asleep." He said: "You never know, you've still got lots of drugs in your system." As soon as he closed the bathroom door, I put the questionnaire in a briefcase I had brought. It was a remnant of my former life, but it had a lock. I locked it and pushed it under the bed.

Eddy came out and said: "You ready?" I said: "Give me just a minute" and walked into the bathroom. The room was so small. I turned on the water and stood there, staring at myself in the mirror. I don't know what I was looking at. I think maybe I was wishing I could disappear through the mirror, but I had spent years trying that as a kid, when I was a little more innocent, and it didn't work. I splashed some water on my face and heard Eddy knock on the door: "You okay?" I said: "Yeah. Be right out." His voice was going to get to me. It was high, nasal and whiny. I walked out and he looked at me with a professional look, like he was assessing me. As we walked out, he said: "When," and then he laughed, "if you are allowed to be here alone, you must remember to always set the security alarm. The code number is the last four numbers of the telephone number. They have surprise inspections of the apartments all the time and if the code isn't set, they put us all on Buddy or even confine us to the apartment." I said: "okay." He looked at me again and said: "You all right, man?" I said: "Yeah. I must look terrible, huh? It's just all new to me, that's all."

We stood on the breezeway and Eddy immediately lit a cigarette. You could tell he was a professional smoker. He got his cigarette out of the pack, lit, and in his mouth in one nearly invisible motion. The Professor was already there: "Eddy, you know you cannot smoke in my car." Eddy smiled and said: "C'mon, it's only a Chrysler. What's the harm?" The Professor looked at me with an exaggerated face of shock and then turned to Eddy: "What's the harm? I will tell you all of the research since 1964 on the harms of smoking cigarettes, will I? No, I do not think I will. Even if you could understand, and I am not sure you could, you would not. You simply want to challenge me with your addiction. Come." Eddy said: "Wait! Where's Paul? I get to smoke until he gets to the car." The Professor said: "He is not coming tonight. Probably because you stink of cigarette smoke." "Professor," Eddy said: "You know he smokes, too." The Professor said: "Yes, but he is not as obnoxious as you. He is a miracle. You are not." I could tell that this was some kind of routine they had worked on which must have become routine to them. I started to pull open the back door and Eddy put his arm on me. "No, no. You sit in the front. I'll sit in back." I started to politely argue with him that since I was the new guy I should be in the back. He started grinning and kept saying, "No, no." I started laughing because he was acting so silly and said: "All right" and I moved to the front seat.

When we were in the car and moving, he put down his window even though it was still insufferably hot. It was one of those windows that would only go down half way but the hot air was pouring into the car. The Professor said: "Eddy, you think you are so smart to sit in the back while pretending to be polite; no? You think I cannot see or smell the noxious odor from your cigarette. Well, I tell you that I do not care if you die, but I can also tell you that your new roommate and I are both worthy of life, even if you do not wish to live. This car is not the Mackinac Bridge and you will put that cigarette out." I didn't know what the reference to the Bridge was but Eddy obviously did and said: "okay, okay, okay." He then took a long, last drag from the cigarette. It was funny looking. The cigarette was in Eddy's mouth, aimed towards the top of the window, while his face was pressed up against the window. He took the longest drag I had ever seen. He then threw the cigarette out and put up the window. The Professor said: "Eddy, you will now please put down the window again, completely exhale and then put the window up again." Apparently, Eddy had this routine down where he held the cigarette smoke in his lungs as long as possible. If this was a sign of his other addictions, he was one hell of an addict.

The Professor was a scary driver, but I didn't feel like I could say anything. I had no idea where we were going. We got on an eight lane freeway very quickly and then it was like destructo-cars. He seemed sober to me, but he drove like he was drunk, weaving in and out traffic with as much thought as if he were playing a video game. He kept up a constant dialogue to which I could not pay attention. Every few seconds he would yell: "Shit!" or "Fucking asshole!" He leaned over to me and looked me right in the eyes. "There is no language like English for swearing, eh! You must know this," he said, and then he was on to the next few feet of open space. Eddy said: "Professor, if you don't calm down, I'm going to smoke. I know it's going to be my last cigarette, but I'll give the blindfold to Ron since he's in the front seat." The Professor leaned over again and laughed. "Ah, yes, I scare my friends from Michigan do I? I thought you were from the Motor Capital of the world? You are not used to a real driver." "Professor," Eddy said, "we make them there to be driven, not wrecked. Now if you had one of the rich kids in here who's daddy owns an insurance company, they might be happy, but I'm not." At that, the Professor just laughed, accelerated and then pulled over to the exit lane and got off the freeway. "Your arguments are pointless. We have arrived."

We were on a four lane road which was apparently the Atlanta strip of fast-food restaurants. He pulled into a steak house. "This is the only restaurant I have found that has decent beef. They don't know how to cook it, of course, but if you give precise instructions to the waiter on how to cook it, you might not have to throw it away. You and Eddy can stay outside and look at the beautiful people while I secure us a table."

With that, he walked inside while Eddy and I stood in the parking lot. On either side of the road there were brilliant neon signs of unreal colors advertising roller skating, dancing bars, hotels and restaurants. It was visually very exciting. Eddy had already done his magic cigarette lighting trick. It was not as hot as when we left but was still very humid. We stood on the curb of the parking lot. He said to me: "How you doing, man?" I looked at him and said: "Okay, I guess. This is still so new. I started the day going from office to office, talked with my case manager, walked back with Brand, Billy and Michael and now I'm here. This time last week I was in a jail cell. It just feels weird. I have no idea what to expect or what the future will be." "You'll be all right, Ron," Eddy said, "just don't rush it. Take it one day at a time. Stay away from Brand. He's bad news."

I looked at Eddy and said: "Yeah, I got the impression you guys don't like each other." He laughed and said: "It's not a question of like. Nothing he says is the truth so it's impossible to have any kind of relationship with him. Plus he's insane." I said: "Isn't that a little harsh?" He said: "No. Let me tell you why. He's right. I'm a horrible drunk. This is the 53rd time I have either been locked up or in a treatment center. I have my Masters degree in counseling and drug addiction counseling. I worked in another treatment center north of Atlanta for over two years until I relapsed and came here. This kind is rare, but I've seen it before. And you can't trust him or tell him anything. Just be careful."

I said: "okay. I will." I wanted to tell him that I wanted

41

everyone to know all about me so that I didn't live with secrets anymore, but I was afraid. I was just beginning to get to know him. He was my roommate and I wanted to live in a secure environment without fear. But now he was telling me not to trust. I had lived my whole life in fear and not trusting. As I looked at the bright neon against the darkness, I could feel that separation talent start to beg attention. I was tired of it too. Eddy looked at me, grinned and said: "I'm probably scaring the shit out of you. Don't worry. If he hits you, he will be immediately discharged and he's got no place to go." I said: "I've got to worry about violence in this place?" Eddy said: "No, don't worry. He's more scared of me, you, the Professor and everybody. And he knows he's got no place to go. He's very treatment wise but he doesn't realize the counselors are on to him. A good counselor can see a guy like him from a mile away. He pays his monthly fee and they keep him here probably hoping against hope that he might catch on to what it is to be a human. He and I share one thing, we've been drunk or fucked up on drugs since elementary school. It's hard to tell what's real for people like us."

The Professor came out, stood next to us and said: "Ah, what a night. What do you call this kind of weather, something to do with the Bahamas?" I smiled and said: "Balmy. The same word we use for crazy people."

Talking With Eddy

The first night that I slept in the apartment my roommate Eddy said: "Hey, man, if I snore too loud, just come over and shake me. I'll turn over and stop snoring." Touch him? While he was sleeping? Was he crazy? "That's okay. I've been told that I snore, too," I responded. "Yeah, well, Lester, that's my last roommate, used to elbow me at least once a night. I really am the snoring champion. The guys in the other bedroom can hear me." I really did not want to go to his bed, in the dark, in the middle of the night. I said: "I'll make you a deal. I'll put up with your snoring if you put up with me listening to the radio all night." He chuckled and said: "No problem. I sure won't be able to hear your radio, but you will be able to hear my snoring."

I was very nervous getting ready for bed, but the great thing was that no one here knew me. I had no preconceptions to deal with. I got into bed first. Eddy was outside smoking a cigarette. I had the radio on, was lying on my side, and the bed lamp, which was always on because the room was so dark, was on. Eddy walked in and said: "What are you reading?" I said: "I'm trying to read this little red book they gave us." He came over to my bed, looked at it and said: "That's the Big Book." I looked at it, and then him, and said: "'Big Book?' It looks pretty small to me. In fact, when they first gave it, I thought it was "Quotations from Chairman Mao."

Eddy laughed and said: "That'd be something, wouldn't it?

God, can you imagine how the southern boys would react to that? My last roommate was a real southern fascist, but I don't think he knew who Chairman Mao was. I don't even think he knew who Mussolini was, but I bet he heard of Hitler."

Eddy looked like a scholar. His shoulders were bent over and he had a full beard which had patches of white on either side of his chin. The hair on his head was black and so shiny it looked like it had just been oiled. The more I looked at him, especially in the dull light of the bedroom, the more I thought he looked like a Hasidic Jew. I always hesitated asking people their religions, probably because I thought most of them were bunk, shallow, hypocritical and designed to reinforce prejudice and hatred. So instead of asking him if he were Jewish, I said: "You got something against Mussolini and Hitler?" Eddy did a double take and then laughed. He said: "Are you Jewish?" I said, "No, but who knows what my father's family could have been in Europe. We were raised Catholic. What about you?" He said: "As white-bread Protestant as you can get. Personally, I don't think I believe in God, or at least I don't think I do. I've tried, but each time I get close to the idea that there's something beyond all this, it just all falls apart on me. What about you?"

"I totally and without equivocation believe in God, which spelled backwards is dog." He looked at me and said: "Well, do you or don't you." I said, "Yes, I do. I'm sorry, but it's hard for me to be serious more than two seconds in a row. Serious thoughts just bring out the comedian in me. I not just believe, I <u>know</u>, within and down to my cells, that there is something 'beyond all this,' as you say. I'm not sure what it is, but it's there. I think George Lucas got it right: it's 'The Force.'" Eddy smiled and said, "Man, I wish I had that confidence, but I don't. And I think I've tried, too. Did you know that 'the Force' comes from Carl Jung?" I thought for a second, "No, but it makes sense. The 'Force' is sort of like the 'collective unconscious.'"

Eddy started getting ready for bed. We were required to make our beds every day. Some guys just threw their covers over their pillows, others, and most especially the dentists, made theirs with great care and precision. My bed-making abilities fell between the two. Eddy said: "Listen, man, don't read that all at once. It's very thickly written. There are layers of meaning in it." "Like the Bible?" I asked. "Yeah," he said. "And for the people in AA, it is the Bible. It has saved lives. I'd be dead without it." I asked him, "If it's saved your life, why are you here?" "Oh," he said, "that's simple. It's like I said to Brand earlier today. You were there. I'm a drunk. I love drinking. I love being drunk. Simple. I just don't like the consequences." "You mean, the hangovers?" I asked. He laughed. "Shit, no. The hangovers are easy to take. I mean being locked up and being in treatment. Not having a life. Divorces. The whole bit. I've got a couple of cases going on up north but my lawyer got me released to treatment instead of going to jail. If I successfully complete treatment, I won't go back to jail."

I was really beginning to like him. He looked like he was my age and even when he spoke about fearful things, like going to jail, he spoke with a level of honesty that I had been avoiding. I was terrified of

45

going to jail. He said: "Why are you here?" The big question. My professional self, the self that could dissemble, splice reality with words and paste it back together again in another, and still be an accurate version of the truth, started to take over. I had to push it back. I could tell him, I thought, but I still hesitated. The fear of being judged and my overwhelming shame took over. I said: "I got in some trouble back home." I didn't say anything else. He said: "Hey, it's okay if you don't want to talk about it. Shit, I remember when I first got in trouble. It's very scary." His honesty was getting to me. I was on the verge of telling him about the drunkenness, the parties, the loneliness, and being so confused about being gay—the incredible shame of not just being who I was, but even trying to find out who I was.

He was standing at his dresser with his shirt off, transferring cigarettes from one red cardboard cigarette box to the other. He was looking at the cigarettes. Just as I was about to speak and start to tell the truth, he said: "It's scary going to jail. The last time I was in jail, I was in a cell with eight other guys and this gay guy was raping and fucking everyone else in the cell. He was huge. That's when I prayed, boy, for him to leave me alone. What a fucking queer." The professional self in me came out with some anger. I said: "What was he in for?" Eddy said: "He killed his whole family: wife, kids and all, with a ball-peen hammer. He was waiting to get transferred to prison. Forever." I couldn't talk to him about this now. He was looking at me. I was lying on my left side with my head held up by my left palm and the little red AA book still held open to my place with my right hand. I looked down at it and then up at Eddy. "I think he was less gay, or 'queer' as you say, then he was a sociopath." Eddy thought for just a second and said: "Yeah, man, I know you're right. It was just very scary. I think that since he and I shared a cell helped my lawyer get me here." I tried to make light of it. "Plus the fact that you're older probably helped protect you from the ball-peen man, too." Eddy looked at me and said: "Just how old do you think I am?" I said, "Well, a little older than me. I'd guess early to mid-fifties." He got upset: "Jesus! I'm 38!" The look on his face was nearly sorrowful. I tried to make up for it: "My age guessing ability is probably one reason I don't work at the county fair. I'm no good at that stuff." He said: "It's okay. I know it's true. My ex-wife and I are the same age and she looks young for her age. We'd be out and people would honestly think I was her father. It's all those years of drinking. They mount up. I've got hepatitis and my liver functions are way off. In fact, next week I've got to get more tests to see if I can stay here or if I have to go back to the hospital. I hate it there. All those crazy people."

"Hey!" I said. "I was one of those crazy people earlier this week!" He laughed and said: "Yeah, I was too, a few months ago. It's just that they are all so 'crispy.' I hear they've got one guy down there right now who has been so fucked up on cocaine that he still can't talk." I knew who he was talking about. I said: "That guy was my roommate for about two minutes. But how do you know about him? I thought who everyone was and where they are is confidential?" He said: "It is, but you hear things." My nerves started to tingle. A gossip network. I said:

47

"How do you find out these things?" He looked at me with a very serious expression and said: "I've got a feeling that you don't need to be sidetracked by gossip right now. You just need to read your book. You'll get into the swing of things as you need to. 'One day at a time.'"

I said: "I'm already getting sick of hearing that saying. But, I read fast. I'll have this book done by tomorrow." Eddy was taking off his pants and actually hanging them up. This surprised me because they were just blue jeans. I said: "Do you iron them too?" He chuckled and said: "No, but we're going to have a surprise inspection tomorrow, and I'm not going to wear them in the morning. Pants on the floor of the closet equal a flunk. We've had two flunks in a row and one more means the whole dome is on buddy. No movies or going out except to the drug store and the grocery store." I asked: "How do you know that we're going to have a 'surprise' inspection tomorrow?" He said: "I just do. Don't worry about it. And don't rush through that book. Take it slow. Read only the first five chapters." "And then," I said, "what should I do?" He answered: "Read the first five chapters again. Keep reading them until I tell you to go on to chapter six. Take your time. It should be months before you read chapter six. And you should read that book every night." "What," I asked, "am I supposed to memorize it?" "Yes, if you want to live."

He lifted his covers, crawled into bed and turned his light off. I asked: "Should I turn my light off, too?" He said: "No. Just tell me where you are in the book." I told him and he said: "Yeah. Let me give you some history." Then, while he was lying in the dark on his back, he gave me the whole history of the people who founded AA. "They were serious drunks, man. I'd feel right at home with them. The only difference is that they 'came to believe.' I have such a hard time with that. You know, it's really such a simple program, you've only got to do two things."

He then rolled over on his side, pulled the covers half way over his head. He said nothing. I said: "okay. I'll bite. What are the two simple things?" He said, through the covers, "They're easy. All you have to do is quit drinking and change the rest of your life." I was taken aback. "Yeah," I said, "that sounds just like what my oldest brother tells his wife all the time: 'Nancy. Just pick six little numbers. That's all, just six." Eddy laughed. "Yeah, the trick, though, is to get the right six. It's the same idea." I thought he was going to say something else, but he didn't. So I kept reading. Within minutes, the loudest, most raucous noise came from underneath his covers. He was right. His snoring was exceptional. My father snored like that. It was so loud that the guys from the other bedroom could hear. Our door was still partially open. Paul, from the other room, came in and said: "We're trying to watch TV so I'm going to close the door." He started a soundless laugh that took over his whole body. "Boy! You're going to have a hard time. Eddy is the nicest guy but the worst snorer. He smiled and said: "We have to have both bedroom doors shut and we usually leave the TV on to help drown him out. Good luck!"

Going to the Grocery Store

Each apartment we lived in had two bedrooms and two baths. There was a living room, an eating area and a corridor kitchen with a pass-through. Some of the apartments got sunshine. My first one didn't. It was at the back of the building. It was so dark inside that there were always artificial lights on.

We had to share cleaning, cooking and shopping chores. There were no rules or guidelines about how to do this except that they had to be done. I was told by my family counselor that she had learned from my sister that I was a very good cook and that I liked to entertain with cooking. She told me that once in the apartment I was not to cook more than once a week. Otherwise, she said, the other patients would use me to do their chores. Cooking and taking care of others was a way of avoiding treatment, she said.

When I got to the apartment, it was clear that none of the other current residents liked to cook or clean. The place looked like a college apartment. There was more dust than counter space would allow so a lot of it flowed over onto the carpet. I looked through the cupboard and refrigerator. There was nothing fresh. There were lots of frozen meat pies and spices. There were all kinds of hot spices. I found out later than opiate addicts love hot, spicy food. Apparently the same cell "receptors" which responded to the opiate drug also responded to hot stuff. Eating hot and spicy was a way of dealing with drug craving. The pots and pans were the very cheap, thin kind that were slightly thicker than aluminum foil. They were all coated with some space-age, stick-free substance that looked like old burned rubber cement.

One of my new roommates was an owner of his own drug rehabilitation clinic. He liked to grill. He had steaks that were weeks old in the back of the refrigerator that I thought he must have forgotten, but when I asked him he said quite seriously: "They're still good. Aged beef is the best." The first thing he said to me when I moved into the apartment was: "I hear you like to cook. Great." I don't know how he knew that, but all the other guys started making deals with me. "If you cook, I'll clean." "If you cook, I'll do your laundry." One night when these little bargainings were going on, Andy walked in and said: "If you cook, I'll eat it," and then laughed. He always got more out of his jokes than anyone else. For a while, I resisted doing the cooking, but after I had tasted the food the others made, I gladly planned and made the meals. I would have said "executed" the meals, but that is exactly what the other guys did, except the Professor.

The Professor could really cook. He cooked so much that I really didn't have to cook more than once every week for community meal. As he got to know me better, he asked me to make the salad and then, as time went on, I progressed to the salad dressing, and eventually a main course. He sure knew his food. I made a dill vinegar dressing. He had not seen me make it, and as he ate it he told me exactly what all the herbs and spices were that I used. I was amazed. He said: "But, of course, these other men know nothing about food. You could have made

51

a salt water dressing and they would have eaten it." Then he laughed: "But, of course, they are American addicts and alcoholics so what do you expect? You are only half-American, though you wish to deny it, which gives you some appreciation of food." The guy that owned the drug rehab clinic said: "Yeah. The professor has gained 40 pounds since he's been here he likes food so much." I looked at the Professor and said: "Is he serious?" Again, he said: "But of course! If I can't take drugs, which I can never do again, I can cook and eat. Food is a drug that society, especially American society, approves. Since I can no longer have the drugs I want, which do keep me thin, I will get fat, obese even, and have a heart attack in the hospital which reported me and then my bowels will loosen—this happens often you know—and I will shit on the fat, ugly nurse who called the chief of surgery. The only thing better would be to watch her clean it up. But, of course, I will either be unconscious or dead. Still, the victory will be mine."

Earlier the Professor had one of his cars brought to him. Either it had fallen upon him, or he took it upon himself, to go to the grocery to shop for his apartment and mine. The first weekend I was there he came to get me and said: "I will be discharged within a month or so. I can tell you will be here a long time." I started to ask how he knew and he said: "Trust me. I know. And you need it. Take your time. You will never have an opportunity to grow or learn like this again. See, people like us never grew up. We are educated, yes. We are smart, yes. You are very smart." My face must have done something because he said: "Don't interrupt. You are very smart. Perhaps it is best that you do not know this. But no matter how smart or educated, we are so immature, and so arrogant, and so privileged that we are dumb. It is the way of the addict. We are the people who used to fight the wars. We would take insane risks and, if we survived, we would win. Society has no use for us now. But, with the overpopulation, there will be other wars, and we will be fed drugs so that the comfortable, country club types will win. It is the way of the world; the way of history. You Americans, and I consider you an American in this, deny this because it seems ugly. If I didn't make so much money here, I would return to Europe. Ah, that is impossible now. My children, too, are Americans and they are so spoiled. The cars, the clubs, the clothes, I cannot combat that. And now I can no longer get high. But I can eat. You will come with me to the grocery, which is a piss-poor excuse for a store in America. Even in a Third World Country the store would be an embarrassment, but we have no choice. After I leave, I can tell that you are the only one who will know what to do about food. So, I pass this along to you."

Each person got a food voucher for $35 a week. The Professor took all of those so that he had $280 a week to spend. Buying in bulk, he explained, allowed us to buy better food. He went back and forth between the apartments pretending to ask, but really telling each person what they were going to eat the next week. He required a list of non-food items, such as paper towels, laundry supplies and toilet paper before each trip. If the list wasn't delivered, then those items were not purchased. He immediately put me in control of my apartment. As we walked to his car he said: "Now go back and tell Paul he must ride with us. We are only allowed off the grounds in groups of three. Paul will come because he wants to marry one of my daughters. As though I would let him or any other addict get near to my family. But I do not want to see all hope taken from him so I let him believe. Also see what is needed. Ask them what sodas and things like that they need. If they do not pay attention to you, then tell them I said they are fucked! They will learn to appreciate you as they do me." Then he laughed and slapped me on the back. I did as he said and the rehab owner said: "Ron, be careful or you'll be taking care of these apartments once the Professor is gone. I'll be gone too and God alone knows what assholes will move in." I returned to the car and repeated what I had been told. The Professor said: "Of course, he is right. There are so many assholes here."

The Professor played very loud salsa music on the way. He kept up a continuous monologue about something, but I couldn't hear him. He was a terrible driver and my eyes were on the road. All I did was smile and make faces in response. Finally, he said: "Too loud? Do not worry. I am a fantastic driver! Some minor scratches, but this is a Chrysler and not my Mercedes, so it does not matter."

We drove along two-lane roads that were very crowded. Atlanta had not kept up with its population. Paul sat in the back and said only: "I'm just along for the ride and to get out of that hell-hole apartment and away from the assholes." By that, I assumed he meant that the Professor and I were not among the assholes. I asked him about that and he said: "Well, you I'm not so sure about, so I'll give you a break. Now that I think about it, the Professor is an asshole." Then he giggled. He said something else and then giggled some more. I couldn't hear him, so I asked him to repeat it. He said: "Never mind" but kept giggling. He raised his right hand and waved it in the air in front of him as though he were pushing something away. He kept giggling and saying, "Never mind. Never mind." He stopped giggling and started snorting, and tears were coming out of his eyes. The Professor looked at me and said: "We have all often wondered what it is that amuses Paul so much. We think nothing but that he is on some drug that the urine screens—the piss tests—cannot find. He will neither tell us what he laughs at or what he is taking. Because of that, he is very unpopular with everyone but me. Not that popularity counts. Indeed, too many of us got into trouble by trying to be popular." The Professor stopped looking at me, looked at Paul in the back seat and said: "Not that you have ever worried about people liking you," to which Paul gave a very quick, succinct and powerful: "Fuck you!" through his snorts.

"Professor, uh, do you think you could keep your eyes on the road?" "Oh, Ron, you are so untrusting. Do not worry. Besides, we are there." I looked around and saw that we were at a very seedy and run-down strip mall which had as many vacant buildings as it did full ones. At one end was a large supermarket which we all toured. Paul did not go in with us; instead he walked down toward a cigar store. "I thought we all had to stay together?" The Professor said: "Of course we are. But Paul does what he wants, and it is too much work to keep him with us at all times. He will go into the cigar store, say nothing, buy six cigars, put one in his mouth and not light it. Then he will find us and put the most peculiar food in the cart. Then we will check out and return. Relax." "What if we are seen by the staff or another patient?" "Again, relax. The staff doesn't want to see us any more than we want to see them. Other patients? Fuck them. They are all worthless. They are addicts! Of course, so are you and I, but we are different." I started grinning and could not stop. This was truly an absurd situation. Well, I couldn't walk 800 miles home, and I didn't even know how to get back to the apartments, so I guess it was time to shop.

The Professor said: "We will not buy beef. I have already told you how the beef in the South is terrible. The pork is okay—I love that phrase, you know it comes from the Second World War?—and the chicken is also acceptable. What do you expect given their clientele? But the fish, especially the salmon, is perfect!" With that he put all of the fingers of his right hand together and kissed his own fingertips saying: "Viola´!" Then he lowered his voice and said, conspiratorially, "Who could figure this? The customers here are not what I would call salmon fans, but then there never is any accounting for taste: Good or bad. Ah, here we are!"

Where we were was in the fish section. There were all kinds of fish on ice. The Professor stared at them with such an intense face. I wondered if he looked that intense when taking his medical exams or when he was making his own drugs. After at least a moment of silence, which seemed like a year given his normal state of constant mouth, he said: "These fillets are the best. We will take them. I will prepare a lime, garlic and herb marinade. I would ask you to start the fire, but that is the only thing some of the other guys do. So for tonight you can relax after we shop." As he said that, Paul walked up, dumped some stuff in the cart, and then walked away again without saying a word. The Professor said: "See. I told you. Crap." I looked at what Paul had put in. There was a can of smoked mussels ("Mealy" the Professor said), some frozen food called "Hot Pockets," ("Horrid. Frozen McDonalds would be better"), canned green asparagus ("A crime to can a noble vegetable. Anyway, they are slimy once canned") and soft margarine ("Strained lard! Not even good lard because there are no meat renderings in it. At least you can make a sandwich with the real thing."). I said that I thought Paul's food was not too weird and the Professor shot me a look of contempt. "Right now I still think you are sophisticated and I treat you as such. Do not change my opinion by asserting yours." I didn't know what to do so I grinned, grabbed the front of the cart and headed down an aisle. The Professor said: "Get what you need." I said: "The apartment needs butter, good olive oil, good bread, and spices that have slightly more subtle flavor instead of hot sauce. I'd also like some of those small bottled Coca Colas."

We went to the aisle that sold soda pop. I said: "These are pretty expensive so let me buy them." He looked at the price and said: "Yes, they are. But you will not pay. The others should have come and they did not, so fuck them. This is the price they pay and the wages you earn for shopping." I said: "That's not a good idea. I don't want to create enemies." The Professor again said: "Fuck them. They could have come." "Professor," I said, "You only asked Paul and I." He started to say something, laughed, and then said: "You are right, of course, but they should have known I was going to go. All right, you can pay. But then you will see that they will drink these and not repay you. Next time we will see how you feel."

The Professor took over the control of the cart and started walking slowly down each aisle. He picked up various items, looked at each closely and then returned it. In one aisle he picked up a glass which had a candle in it. On the outside was a picture of the Virgin Mary with the Infant Jesus in her hands. He stared at it so long I thought he was going to buy it or that he was very religious. When he put it back I asked: "You don't want it?" "No," he said. "Then why did you look at it so long?" "I was just wondering why people buy shit like that. Only poor people do. It's a shame. But they are the same people I prescribe for so I must understand the culture."

When we got to the produce department the Professor said: "They have vine ripened tomatoes. They are very expensive, yes? But how else can you make a salad or salsa. California has wrecked the idea of fresh. The vegetables look wonderful but taste like cardboard. Why they have such tomatoes in a store like this is a mystery to me, but it is also a mystery why someone would spend nearly ten dollars to buy a glass worth a quarter with a picture of a white virgin. She was a Jewish child from the Middle East. She probably had acne, bad teeth and bad breath. I am Catholic and I say this. But we true Catholics know that what is presented is not always that which is. It is like the tomatoes. The

California ones look perfect and, like the image on the glass, have no depth or substance. It is not in the image of perfection that we find God and truth, it is in our pain. And we addicts and alcoholics are very familiar with pain. We have run from it so long, but once we embrace it we find truth, faith and the will to live. After all, what does that obnoxious director at the clinic say? We have been slowly, or not so slowly, committing suicide, which is a sin. Yes, this is true though he knows nothing of sin. He is a dentist after all: Neither a philosopher nor a doctor. But he is one hell of an addict." He stopped talking and looked over at the open case which displayed the green vegetables. "Now there is the noble asparagus." He walked to it, picked up a stalk and snapped it. "Hear how sharp the snap sounded? It is fresh. We will quickly steam it but not so that it is cooked through. Then we will marinate it in olive oil, a little butter, a little lemon and then grill it. We could put tarragon with it, but tarragon can be overpowering." I suggested that it would be pure without any herbs. "Yes, he said, "It will be delicious!" Then he said, darkly as though he were telling me a deep secret, "You know, of course, that your roommates wouldn't know tarragon from basil. You must be careful."

I wasn't sure if he meant I should be careful of herbs, or my roommates, or why their lack of knowledge of herbs meant I should be careful, so I just smiled, raised my eyes and walked to the onions and garlic.

The cart was full but Paul had not yet come back. The Professor said we should go to the checkout. "No matter what is said, be polite to the checkout clerks." I said: "Why." He said: "Just listen and say nothing." The checkout counters were dirty and peopled by high-schoolers. There were all kinds of newspaper pages full of coupons on the floor. There were unfinished displays of soda pop and fast foods crowding the aisle. Most of the employees were centered around one cashier at her counter, giggling and loudly repeating popular one-liners to whatever she was saying. The Professor chose her aisle, probably because she was the only clerk next to a register.

She was probably about seventeen, and she obviously preferred to check out the bagger instead of us, but when she finished, she announced the total. The Professor smiled a huge smile and handed her the vouchers which the center had given us. "Oh," she announced to anyone within hearing distance with a look of amusement and disgust, "more addicts!" I was really surprised, but the Professor kept smiling. He pushed his glasses up on his nose with his middle finger and said to her: "Yes. We are here." She said: "Hmmm." She looked at us with a long look of disbelief and judgment, as though we had discovered a great scam and she was jealous that she wasn't part of it. "Hard to believe you're addicts with those little polo ponies on your shirts and those German sandals. The addicts I know don't have teeth, and they come in here at night to take the papers with them to use as blankets."

The Professor said: "Yes, it is a terrible disease. It is hard to say how anyone will be treated by it. Perhaps someone in your family is so afflicted? If so, I can direct him or her to a truly fantastic treatment center, though, of course, the cure is not guaranteed. One must learn to deal with these things and afflicted people with great patience, tolerance and love. Don't you agree?"

Sunday Twice Spiritual

On every Sunday, at 9:00 a.m., exactly, each dome had to hold its own "spiritual," which consisted of all of us being together and contributing something "spiritual" to the group. The time was set by the rules and no one was allowed to be late. We gathered together out on the walkway at 9:00 a.m. If someone tried to sleep in on the only day we could, one of the more eager patients, whom I later found out were called Rule Nazis, would get a gleeful smile and go wake the offender, threatening to tell the counselor on call that Mr. X was going to be three minutes late. One guy came down in short "jammies," which looked like something his mother gave him for his birthday. Most of the guys came out in messy T-shirts and athletic wear which had been carpeting their floors for a while, with their hair all askew and saying only three words to the group, all in the inquisitive mode: "Cigarette? Light? Coffee?" Not quite spiritual, but consciousness comes first, then realization, then enlightenment. Along the way are all kinds of temptations, addictions and assholes.

I was nervous my first Sunday. I only had two books with me. One was the most recent Stephen King horror thriller. I didn't think it appropriate to read a passage which would send only shivers of terror among the group when what was being sought were passages of guidance and comfort. The other was a book with letters by Abraham Lincoln. I found one which I thought was appropriate. I asked Eddy if it would be okay and he said, "Hey, man, read what you want. I don't care if you read the phone book."

Mike, the senior addict, was the last man out. He was supposed to lead us, but he was busy making early morning jokes, talking about golf, tennis, and what the Professor was going to cook for dinner. It seemed to me that everyone was enjoying this. It was warm but not yet too hot to be outside. Actually, it was disconcerting. There was barbed wire on top of a cyclone fence, but just a few feet away there were song birds, sunlight and jokes. I started to feel pretty comfortable.

Brand, though, did not look comfortable. He sat straight up in a chair against the wall. It really looked like he had a two by four down his back. He looked straight ahead but at nothing. His face was white and he was tightly clutching four thin paperback books. He started clenching his jaw. Eddy went back into the apartment and Brand said: "Hey, you can't go back into the apartment until Spiritual is finished." Eddy said: "Then I guess it's finished, because I'm going to get more coffee." Brand started to say something else, but Eddy went to the door, which was only about four feet away, and left it open. Everyone got quiet. Mike crossed one leg on top of the other, leaned on the knee of the upper one, took a drag from his cigarette and said: "Brand, you sure know how to bring your higher power into this." Eddy came back out and said: "Yeah, and I think his higher power is Heinrich Himmler." There were some laughs at this, but some of the other guys were clearly uncomfortable. Brand said: "Well, at least I got a higher power, Eddy." Mike said: "Enough. Let's go. Someone start."

A guy I hadn't met yet cleared his throat and said: "My name is Tony, and I'm an alcoholic and an addict." Everyone said: "Hello, Tony," and Eddy immediately said: "Will you guys stop it? This isn't a meeting. You don't have to introduce yourself every time you say something." Tony said: "Well, if I can receive Eddy's blessing to speak, then maybe I will also receive it when I speak. We have new guys here, and I was just trying to be courteous to them." He leaned forward as he said this and looked at the concrete walk. He put his head down as if he were saying a prayer and said in a supplicating and sarcastic voice: "So, Eddy, if I can receive your permission, I will proceed. But if you don't want me to talk, then I won't. My Higher Power already knows what's in my heart." Eddy said: "Yes, Tony, he does. And so do we. The question is if you do. Why don't you look at me just once?" "What for," Tony said. "So you can bite my head off the rest of the way?" Mike said: "Tony, no one is trying to bite your head off. And, Eddy, just shut up for once. Okay?" Eddy said: "Sure, but I've got to be honest about my feelings and I just don't like passive-aggressive liars." No one said anything, and Mike took a long drag on his cigarette and grinned as he slowly exhaled. I was looking at Billy who looked back at me as if to say: "What's going on here?" Mike said: "Well, maybe we can all look at ourselves instead of others for a while."

No one said anything and Tony cleared his throat again. "Well, okay, now that I've received the blessing of silence from Eddy's 'Higher Power' I'll go on. There are many saint days and today is one of them, but it's an obscure one for most of you. Well, that was a presumption, wasn't it? I should say, I expect it is obscure for most of you. In my church, we bless the animals. My beloved wife and I take our animals to church every year on this day and they are blessed by the minister. Of course, our animals are leash trained and not everyone's animals are, and they still bring them even though they've been told not to, and there are even notices in the bulletin weeks ahead of time saying 'don't bring them to church unless they are leash trained,' which would, of course, be hard to do with a horse or cow, but most people just bring their dogs and cats, though some bring their birds, so I suppose there is an exception for birds since they are brought in their cages, and there aren't any leashes small enough for them anyway, unless of course they have an eagle or vulture or some other large bird, but...." Mike interrupted him and said: "Tony...." "Yes, yes, I know. Back on track? Right? The king of parenthetical remarks. Right? Well, not lots of these southerners know about this."

I was taken aback. Why would he assume that none of us knew about St. Francis? And why would he throw in that comment about southerners?

Tony continued: "Well, St. Francis blessed the animals and many churches continue that practice. I don't know if the Catholics do, even though he was a Catholic, but my church does and I want to read St. Francis' prayer. The minister says this every year over the assembled animals. It's so beautiful that my beloved wife and I cry each time because our animals are so precious to us. I don't suppose any of the rest of you feel close to your pets but ours are more than pets, they are members of our family...." Mike again said: "Tony." I wondered why Tony would make such assumptions. My dogs, Tuck and Dora, kept me alive. I had a photograph of them in my wallet. I looked around and Billy was looking at me smiling. He knew my dogs were important to me.

Tony continued: "Well, since it's obvious that my time is being cut short, just let me read the prayer. If some of you get it, fine, but I really do feel like I'm talking to the air. He then read the prayer:

> Lord, make me a channel of thy peace—that where there is hatred, I may bring love—that where there is wrong, I may bring the spirit of forgiveness—that where there is discord, I may bring harmony—that where there is error, I may bring truth— that where there is doubt, I may bring faith—that where there is despair, I may bring hope—that where there are shadows, I may bring light—there where there is sadness, I may bring joy. Lord, grant that I may seek rather to comfort than to be comforted—to understand, than to be understood—to love, than to be loved. For it is by self-forgetting that one finds. It is by forgiving that one is forgiven. It is by dying that one awakens to Eternal Life. Amen.

Paul was next. He was a smoker, too, and put his still-lit cigarette in the ashtray and said: "Don't none of you thieves take that. Who's got a 24 Hour?" One of the guys threw him a small black book and he said: "Okay, here's the thought for today. I'll leave the meditation and prayer for someone else who doesn't have the book." He read from the book, which took about 20 seconds, grinned, threw the book back, and grabbed his cigarette and said: "Now, all the rest of y'all think about that."

I was confused again. I thought this was serious business. For all Tony's parentheticals, he obviously had spent some time thinking about what he was going to say. Paul didn't seem to care. It went like this through the rest of the guys. Few of them were paying attention to anyone's presentation. Some got up and got coffee. Others shifted in their chairs and some actually got up and walked around until it was Billy's turn. Mike said: "Hey, c'mon guys. There's no tennis, or golf, or TV until this is done. Go ahead, Billy."

Billy said: "I'm not Christian, but I do like something from the Bible, which I've memorized. Actually, I won a contest in second grade for having memorized it:

> The Lord is my shepherd; I shall not want.
>> He maketh me to lie down in green pastures:
>> he leadeth me beside the still waters.
>
> He restoreth my soul: he leadeth me in the
>> paths of righteousness for his name's sake.
>
> Yea, though I walk through the valley of
>> the shadow of death, I will fear no evil:
>> for thou art with me; thy rod and
>> thy staff they comfort me.
>
> Thou preparest a table before me in the
>> presence of mine enemies; thou anointest
>> my head with oil; my cup runneth over.
>
> Surely goodness and mercy shall follow me
>> all the days of my life; and I will dwell in
>> the house of the Lord forever.

No one moved when he was speaking. His head was level when he spoke, but his eyes were fixed and focused on something the rest of us couldn't see. He spoke slowly, calmly and with deep conviction. It was obvious this wasn't a mere recitation, but rather a heart-felt prayer. When he was finished, no one said anything.

Then it was Brand's turn. He said: "Well, I guess I'm one of those southern boys Tony talked about. I don't know about all that fancy stuff about blessing animals. That seems silly to me. Animals are for hauling, hunting or eating. But I've got four books here...." Mike interrupted and said: "We've been through this. You only get to read from one." Brand said: "Well, they've all got good stuff in them this bunch of alcoholics need to hear." Mike said: "We're all more likely to listen to one if we don't have to hear them all. And you know the rule. Since you like rules for others so much, why don't you obey one yourself?"

"All right. All right. But the counselor on call is going to hear how you've violated my free speech rights." Eddy said: "You don't have free speech in jail or psychiatric hospitals, Brand, and your jail released you to this psychiatric hospital, so just get on with it. It's going to sound like a Hallmark greeting card anyway."

Brand said: "Well, I know who's going to Hell here pushing away the Lord and all." Mike started to say something and Brand said: "Just give me a minute to figure out which one to read." He sat silently and went through each book, which he had marked with bright yellow

Post-It notes. "Okay. Here it is." He read slowly and needed prompting with some of the words. It was obvious this was a routine ritual, the arguing, the prompting and Brand's self-satisfied smile. I don't remember what he read, but my impression of what he read is clear. It was something about the warmth of sunshine and how it made him feel good. Tony was right. It was a Hallmark greeting card.

The Professor was next. He said: "It's not for me to take another person's inventory." He paused and then looked at me and Billy. "That means to judge. We are not to judge another person's recovery or life. Jesus told us that but so many persist in saying Jesus' name while they act like Herod. And you know the recovery way of saying 'do not judge.' For those of you who have forgotten, it is this: 'If I haven't taken my personal inventory today, then I ought not to take yours. If I have taken mine, then I can't take yours.' This bickering must stop or you will risk my recovery, and I am so selfish that I will not let you do that. I see that Mike is looking at me to stop so I will, but not before I read what Bill W., the founder of this program, the savior of us, wrote about fighting. Listen to this my friends.'

> We have ceased fighting anything or anyone—even alcohol. For by this time sanity has returned. We can now react sanely and normally, and we find that this has happened almost automatically. We see that this new attitude toward liquor is really a gift from God.
>
> That is the miracle of it. We are not fighting it; neither are we avoiding temptation. We have not even sworn off. Instead, the problem has been removed. It does not exist for us. We are neither cocky nor are we afraid.
>
> That is how we react—so long as we keep in fit spiritual condition.

Since I was sitting next to the Professor, I was next. I said: "I don't have a religious or spiritual book. I don't even have a Bible here. I hardly know who Bill W. is. All I have is Stephen King and letters from Abraham Lincoln. One of his letters was written on July 22, 1860, to a guy named George Latham who had wanted to get into Harvard, but was rejected. It's about how perseverance is important, but so is knowing what you really want. Then I read.

My dear George

I have scarcely felt great pain in my life than on learning yesterday from Bob's letter that you had failed to enter Harvard University. And yet there is very little in it, if you will allow no feeling of *discouragement* to seize and prey upon you. It is a *certain* truth, that you *can* enter and graduate in, Harvard University; and having made the attempt, you must succeed in it. *"Must"* is the word.

I know not how to aid you, save in the assurance of one of mature age, and much severe experience, that you *can* not fail if you resolutely determine that you *will* not.

The President of the institution can scarcely be other than a kind man, and doubtless he would grant you an interview and point out the readiest way to remove or overcome the obstacles which have thwarted you.

In your temporary failure there is no evidence that you may not yet be a better scholar, and a more successful man in the great struggle of life, than many others who have entered college more easily.

Again I say let no feeling no discouragement prey upon you and in the end you are sure to succeed.

With more than a common interest I subscribe myself, Very truly your friend.

The Professor looked at me and said: "That is good. Too often we think recovery can only be found in the recovery culture. To be successful, we must find it in everyday life, in everything we do. It will not be all that long until we are all released from here back into the 'real world.' At that time, we will need all the inspiration we can find."

Mike said: "okay. Let's close." At that everyone stood up and formed a rough circle. Each guy put his arms around the guy next to him. Some reached across the guy they stood next to in order to put their hands on another guy. I didn't know what was going on but put my arms on those next to me. Mike looked at everyone, letting his face linger on Brand's and Tony's. Then he said: "Okay guys, the Serenity Prayer." With that, everyone said: "God, grant me the serenity to accept the things I cannot change, the courage to change the things I can, and the wisdom to know the difference."

The group broke up. Eddy came over to me and started to say something, but before he could, Brand said very loudly: "Ron, I don't care what the Professor says. You ain't gonna recover if you don't read recovery literature. And I don't know about the rest of the guys, but reading a letter from Lincoln down here is a little insulting. You in Georgia now, boy! Of course, you're new at this, but Tony should have known better. Imagine, blessing dogs!"

"Brand, I don't know you at all," I said, "but I want to tell you a really important thing about the secret of spirituality." Brand looked at me, not trusting at all, but eager to hear what I was going to say.

"What?" he said. "Dog spelled backwards," I said, "is God." He looked at me as if I were an idiot. Later on Eddy said that was his look when he was trying to spell.

Eddy steered me into the apartment where he said: "Be careful. I think it's one thing for me to taunt Brand, because I've been here and I'm a drunk. I'm sure you're a drunk, too, but not like any he's ever seen." I didn't say anything. Mike walked in. He got a huge grin when he saw me and said: "Oh, I don't know, Ron, here less than a week and already you're identifying the nuts. Be careful, though. If you keep talking to Brand like that, you're going to put his brain into gear lock. No telling what he'll do then. But he hates Tony and Eddy much more than he hates you, so you'll probably be all right until they leave."

I was getting scared and said so. Mike said: "Don't worry. Just don't make him your friend. He's got lots of issues." "Yeah," I said, "I sensed some of them." Mike said: "Before I got suspended, I practiced psychology for 20 years and saw lots of men like him. None of them get cured. It's just a question of how long they will stay in treatment. Of course, there are always miracles." I said: "I'd like a few." Mike said: "Well, you'll hear about the promises and how they come true, and they do if you let them. Me, this is my third try to stay sober. Well, I'm going to play golf. See you guys at dinner." With that, he walked back outside.

Eddy sat down on a chair and said to me: "What are your plans?" I sat on a couch next to him and said: "Plans? None. You tell me, I guess." Eddy said: "Usually guys use Sundays to write their First Step, but you just got here, so if I were you I'd read some of the Big Book, take a nap and then after dinner we go to spiritual." "Isn't that what we just had?" I asked. He said: "Yeah, but on Sunday night we have to go to either an AA meeting or a spiritual which is run by Father Liam. Have you met him yet?"

"I'm not sure," I said. Eddy said, "Well, you should have met him in the hospital. He runs a morning program there each day." "Is he a short Irish priest" I asked? Eddy said: "Yeah." "I saw him there, but I didn't like him," I said. Eddy looked at me with an expression of surprise on his face. I continued: "I was raised Catholic and don't have much use for priests. Why is he here anyway?" Eddy said: "Most people like him a lot. I guessed that you would too. That's one thing you and Brand have in common. He can't stand Father Liam. He's here on some kind of assignment. We're his parish for a while. I think he's doing both penance and service. He had a huge drinking problem, and once he got sober and was in the program a while he started doing volunteer work here to help the spiritual side of the program. He wound up being on staff. That happens a lot. Half the staff are drunks. Well, it takes one to know one."

Eddy then said: "Look'it, I've got a day pass and I'm going to see my ex-wife. We're not supposed to leave you in the apartment, but the Professor will be across the way. Just leave the door open. You'll be okay. I'll be back about five."

He left, so I went into our bedroom, turned on the light and started to read the Big Book. Some of it was hard to understand, but it was interesting. It had an awful lot of material about a "higher power." I got lost in the book and started thinking about home, why I was where I was, how alone I felt, and my dogs. Then I started to cry. I turned over on my side and fell asleep. About three o'clock I heard someone in my room. I looked up. It was one of the guys from the morning spiritual who had had on jammies. He had an acoustic guitar in his hands. He said: "Hey, sorry to wake you up. I'm Tory. I hear you play a little guitar, and I thought you might like this for company. I'll leave it here. You just go back to sleep and maybe you'll want to play a little when you wake up." He turned around and left.

I sat up and looked at the guitar. I used to play a lot, but I hadn't played seriously in years and hardly at all since I started drinking heavily. I picked it up and started fingering the strings. I must have been louder than I thought because the Professor walked in and said: "If you play, you must play for all of us. Come outside with me. Anyway, Brand has been gone, but he is due back, and if you are alone he will make a secret call reporting all of us. I am sure he must have been a Gestapo in a former life and he is being punished by being given the life he has now. Why we are being punished by having to associate with him I don't know. It is one of those mysteries for which we should be grateful." I said, "Are you serious?" He laughed and said: "I don't know. It could all be bullshit, because he really is such an asshole."

I went back out on the porch and sat where I had that morning. Tory and Billy were sitting out there too. Billy was smoking. Tory was leaning back against the wall, still with his jammies on, his hands intertwined behind his head. Neither was saying anything. I picked some old songs. Neither Billy nor Tory said anything, but both started singing to the songs I was playing. They both had amazingly good voices. I was jealous about that because my voice on a good day sounded like Bob Dylan on a very bad day. I started smiling. I wish I had been able to do this in college, sitting around playing the guitar with what appeared to be some regular guys. We did this for about forty-five minutes. Then Doug, one of Brand's roommates, came down. He said: "Hey! Y'all sounding like shit. Let me have that guitar and show you a few things." Without looking, Tory said: "No. That's my guitar and you ain't playing it unless you can pay for it, which I happen to know you can't." I started to hand it back to Tory, saying: "Yes, it is expensive. Thanks for letting me play it." Tory said: "Ron, it pleases me so much to hear you play it, so I'd be obliged if you'd keep it for a while." I asked "Don't you want to play it?" He said, "Yeah, but I can't. My drugs of choice have turned my brain into plastic. It's hard enough to zip my pants and button my shirts, which is why I wear these jammies as much as I can. Nothing but holes and elastic, and it's still hard for me to get dressed. I was in detox for over a month and they only sent me up here because they were getting tired of seeing me drool and fall on my face when I tried to out of bed. Y'all keep it for a while." I didn't know the history between Tory and Doug so I just kept it and strummed very quietly.

The Professor came out of his apartment and said: "What has happened to the music? I need it! No one went to the grocery and we have only chicken! I hate chicken! There is nothing to do with it!" I saw this as an excuse to quit playing and get away from Tory and Doug. The tension between some of these guys reminded me of home. I said: "Let me see what you've got in your kitchen."

The Professor and I went into his apartment. There were all kinds of spices, hot sauces and bags of rice. I said: "What is it with the hot sauces?" He looked at me and said "You don't know? The opiate addicts love their food hot. The hotter the better." I said: "Why?" He said: "The chemicals from the hot sauces interact with the same receptors as do the opiates. It's a safe way of satisfying their cravings. There is some pain and pleasure in it. The hot sauces or spices are hot and painful to eat, yet they activate endorphins which are very pleasurable. You can tell the drug of choice from the cravings. Chocolate and sweet things are the choice of alcoholics, but chocolate will trigger cravings of crack addicts. It is all so interesting."

I said: "I'm not into hot sauces." The Professor laughed and said: "Well, as they say in the program...not yet! But we have nothing decent to eat, and if I have to give up drugs I will not give up food!" He laughed and said: "Of course, I will never again trust an addict, but what am I saying? I am an addict! Of course, though, with the exception of you, these other addicts are all so crass."

While he was talking, I looked around the little kitchen. There were also about five kinds of mustard, including dry mustard, some real cream, onions, garlic and a real cast iron pan. I asked the Professor: "If I cook, will you clean?" He said, "If you cook, I will clean. If I don't clean, I will get one of those lazy addicts to clean." I said: "This will be messy, but I will make you pan-fried chicken with mustard sauce with onions and garlic over rice. Now get out of the kitchen." The Professor said, "I will watch you, of course!" I said: "okay but get out of the kitchen."

As I cooked, the Professor kept up a dialogue of gossip, information, accusation, innuendo and warning. "One of the men this morning used to be a prostitute. I won't tell you whom so that you have no prejudices. I, of course, have none. We will all do anything to get drugs. I cannot say that he is gay, but if he is, it is a genetic status, like hair color or height. Why are you Americans so uptight about sexuality? You define who you are on an insignificant part of your behavior. You are so much more forgiving of violence, even murder, than you are of what goes on in a bedroom, yet you are so fascinated by both."

I was so tempted to tell him about me, my fears and why I was there. I started to say something but he was caught up in what he was saying. "You know, the opiate addicts are so cold for so long when they start to withdraw. One member of our group wore a wool overcoat in the middle of summer in Georgia! Because he was so cold! Amazing! Still, it is the drugs which does that." I couldn't see him, but he was obviously looking at me. "Ah! You create such a mess. I will not clean, but I will make sure someone does. I will choose Brand perhaps. Though he is dangerous, he needs discipline. But if I ask him to clean, I must ask him to eat with us, which I will not do. I don't really want him here anyway. You would be well advised to stay clear of him. He and Eddy hate each other and Brand is so sick he will blame you for his feelings about Eddy and Eddy's feelings about him. He, I mean Brand, is so very sick. I know! I will ask Eddy and Paul. They are both fairly civilized and love to eat. They will clean." As I was sautéing the garlic and onions he said: "It is beginning to smell tolerable. Let us see what you can do with nothing."

I smiled because he was so funny without meaning to be. He caught me and said: "You think I am funny? So does Kathy. If I start to say something, she just laughs. Some of the sicker patients of this wonderful place think that she is having an affair with a patient, which is, of course, impossible. They will not say who. She is a total professional. I know she would not cross that line. And if she did, her affair would be with me, and since it is not, she is touching none of us." I laughed more as I transferred the onions and garlic to a dish. I put olive oil in the cast iron pan and turned the heat up as high as it would go. I also turned the oven on. I said: "And if she wanted to mess around with a patient, it would be you because you are so perfect; right?" The Professor laughed again and said: "Yes! Me! The perfect addict!"

At that Eddy walked in and said: "You mean the perfect asshole." Eddy said: "What are you doing?" I replied: "Cooking your dinner in exchange for you cleaning." He said: "I'll clean anytime you want to cook." The Professor loudly interjected: "No! Cooking for others is a treatment issue with Ron. He can only cook once a week. Eddy, not cleaning is an issue for you, so you can clean all week." He laughed again. It was fun, real fun, to see a guy who got so much humor out of being himself.

Eddy said: "Why are you frying chicken with the oven on?" The Professor answered for me. "Eddy, you are still addled. It is obvious. He is browning the chicken in the cast iron pan you see in front of you with your very own eyes. He will then place the chicken in the baking dish you also see with your very own eyes, with the equally obvious sautéed onions and garlic with the sauce he has yet to make. And, of course, the trick will be in the sauce. So we still are holding our judgment of Ron in reservation."

Eddy said: "Professor, talk about treatment issues. Your judgment makes the Puritans look like California liberals. You need to bring this up in group."

I put the chicken in the baking dish with the onions and garlic on top. Then I took the pan off the stove and started mixing the mustards in the pan itself. The mustards all sizzled and then boiled. I threw some of the dry mustard in just to do it. Some risky behavior, but, what the hell! I said: "This is the first time I've cooked anything in a very long time without wine and vodka. The wine for the food and the vodka for me." I was an addict too! Welcome home! Eddy said: "Oh, oh! I think he's screwing it up!" I said: "Lay off. It's only mustard. The cream and the butter will be the trick." As I said that, I tested the pan to see if it had cooled down enough to mix the sauce. It had and I did. I put it back on the heat until it started to simmer and then poured it over the chicken, and then I put the whole mess into the oven. I started cooking the rice. Once it was on I said: "okay. It's time for the first stage of cleanup." Eddy started to protest, but the Professor said: "It is like the founding of the colonies here. There are no slaves so if you eat, you must contribute. Clean Eddy." I thought that was an odd remark and said so. The Professor said: "Really, Ron, if you know anything about the history of your country, you must know that it could not have been built without enslaving one race and nearly exterminating another. The naiveté of Americans is amazing. They refuse to admit they like to have sex or get high. You have built a whole culture on hypocrisy."

Neither Eddy nor I said anything. I sat down on his couch and said, "Well, Professor, since I cooked and Eddy is cleaning, perhaps you could prove the sincerity of your egalitarian remarks by setting the table." He laughed and said: "Of course! But you will be disappointed to know that we only have paper napkins. It is such a discomfort, but who would iron them if they were linen or cotton?" Eddy and I started laughing. The Professor said: "Well, Ron, even you are not through. Go get my roommates and the remainder of yours so that we can eat as a family, which we are, of course. All diseased, all liars, with only the grace of God to sustain us."

By the time I found everyone and got them to the Professor's, it was time to eat. He had put together a small salad. He and I put the food on the plates and served everyone. He, Eddy, Paul and I got to sit at the table because we had cooked, cleaned, or in Paul's case, there was a promise to clean. Paul looked at the food and, bringing the plate to his face, smelled it. "What the hell is this?" he said. The Professor said: "It is actually chicken de jon. If you do not like it, you can throw it at Ron and he will clean. Now, let us pray and then all try the experiment." He led us in a very heartfelt prayer, asking for God's blessing of the food and each of us. He concluded: "And, God, most of all, please bless Brand. He needs you more than the rest of us combined." Eddy looked at the Professor, who mocked a look of surprise and said: "Eddy, that is not judgment, that is a prayer." I said: "Or, as we lawyers would say, a 'request for relief.'" Nearly everyone laughed at that and the Professor said: "Exactly!"

The Professor tasted the food and said: "Excellent! I am proud of you. Of course, you are half Hungarian. No American could have made this out of nothing." We all laughed and Mike said: "Professor, why don't you eat and stop talking. We'll all spend some quiet time imagining what you'd say." The Professor said: "But of course! Even I am too much, too magnificent, for me to talk for a long period of time."

When we were nearly done, Eddy said: "Ron, go grab two cushions off the couch. We've got to get going to Spiritual with Father Liam." I had no idea why we would need couch cushions but went to our apartment to get them. By the time I got back outside, the Professor was arranging transportation. "Ron, Eddy, Billy and Paul will ride with me. The rest of you will walk or arrange your own transportation." We got in his car and drove to campus.

Once we got there, we parked and walked into the building. There were two security guards watching us. I said: "Eddy, why are they looking at us?" He answered: "They memorize the pictures of the patients and then make a list of those who didn't come. If you don't come here, you have to go to an AA meeting with at least two other people who then have to verify where you were. If you're not at either, you can be sent back to the hospital. No one wants that, because it costs a thousand dollars a day and you're back where you started. 'Do not pass go and do not collect one hundred dollars."

We walked into the all-purpose room. Eddy grabbed a chair and told me to grab one. He placed his on its back and then pushed his cushion into it. He then laid down, using the cushion as a pillow and the chair as support. I did the same thing.

Father Liam was already there at the front of the room on the small stage. He had a small portable stereo with him. Various patients were talking with him and though I could not hear what they had to say, nearly everyone near him laughed when he said something. After a few minutes, all of the chairs were on their backs with patients leaning on them or lying underneath them.

Father Liam then said: "Are we all here? We'd better be or some of us will be in jail!" His laughter was loud and it almost sounded like a cackle. "All right. For those of you who are new, this is Sunday Spiritual. Now remember, this is an incredible luxury for all of you. Instead of the moaning I hear, you should all be grateful for this luxury.

After all, this is an insane asylum for the rich. Sixty years ago, they would have stripped you down, hosed you down and locked you up!" He had a gleeful look on his face. He looked at me and said: "Get comfortable." I laid back and looked at the ceiling. He said: "That's right. Now someone get the lights." The overhead fluorescent lights went off and there were only two side lights on.

"Tonight I want to talk about grieving and remembering the dead. We all have such pain and sorrow in our lives. That's one reason we are addicts and alcoholics. We are super sensitive to pain and to loss. Colors are brighter for us. Sounds have more layers. Sometimes this is too much so we dull our senses with drugs and alcohol. We don't want to feel, so we turn ourselves off.

"An example of this is when someone we love dies. Of course, being addicts and alcoholics we only tell people we love them when we are loaded or after they are gone. Then we treasure every moment we bitched about when our loved one was alive. We never live in the present. We only live in the past or in the future. It is easier to deal with someone after they are dead."

I thought of my brother-in-law who had recently died. I was glad the lights were dim because I started to cry. I had never told him I loved him. Though I told people how much I had loved him, I never told him. I didn't even acknowledge his death to myself until a few months after he died. I had sat on the top of my new stove, which was glass topped, and which cracked under my weight. I immediately grabbed the telephone to call him and ask him what to do. As I dialed, I realized he would not pick up the phone. He would not be there. And then I sat on the broken stove top, on the broken glass, and bawled.

"I never told my mother I loved her," Father Liam said. "I hated dealing with her. She was a tiny woman. In Ireland, everyone was poor unless you were English, which we were not. We never had any money or fancy food. Yet once a week she made this special bread from nothing. It was delicious. She had a special way of cutting it. She looked at it as if she loved it. Then she would sharpen her knife. With her left hand, she would hold the loaf just so, and with the tenderness you would use to wipe a child's chin, she sliced that bread and quietly sang to herself.

"She died when I was here in America. I flew back to Ireland for her funeral and didn't cry. I drank but could not get drunk. A few years after her death, I was in a bakery in downtown Atlanta and I saw an old man cut a loaf of bread the same way she did. I couldn't move. I was transfixed by the sight. Being Irish, I thought this was a sign that God was going to strike me dead for not loving her. But then I realized it was a gift from God. He had given me the opportunity to see my mother in the life of someone else."

I wasn't the only one crying now. There were sobs from all over the floor. Eddy was on one side of me, but I didn't know who was on the other. The other person was crying and sobbing audibly.

Father Liam continued: "As we play the music tonight, think of how you can see the faces of your missing loved ones -- they don't have to be dead -- in the faces and actions of others. Think about how you wish you could have expressed your love. Think about how you can express your love now. Let yourself be in touch with your Higher Power."

He then said "lights" once again and all the lights went out. The only lights on were the fire exit lights. He must have started his little stereo because music started playing. The music wasn't songs, it was sounds of various instruments without any true melody or obvious structure. I took a deep breath and iistened. As I did so, I saw the face of my dead brother-in-law. I saw my father, now also dead. I saw a young friend who had died in a car accident. I cried even more. I felt guilty that I hadn't told them I loved them. I felt selfish that I had taken their attentions for granted.

This must have gone on for about half an hour. The music quietly died and no one said anything. Liam then said: "After I saw that man cut his bread, I went out to my car and sat alone. I started talking to my mother. I said 'I love you. I always loved you.' She spoke back to me. She told me she loved me too. She loved me when she made the bread. She loved me when she cut and served the bread. She loved me when she disciplined me. She loved me when she was harsh with me. I told her I realized that she loved me as she could. I thanked her for the gift of life and that I felt compassion for her trials, for her anger, and for the limitations life gave her and the limitations she gave herself."

He stopped talking. Then a patient said: "I never told my daughter I loved her. She died when she was seventeen in a car accident. She was drinking and ran into a tree. She...." The patient stopped talking but started sobbing. There was silence for a few minutes except for the crying, sobbing and sniffing. Then someone with a younger voice said: "I always hated my parents. They had extra marital affairs and never spent time with us. I had to raise my brothers and sisters. Until tonight I never thought that they could have their own problems."

It went like this with people giving a few thoughts about people they had loved who were gone, either by death or distance. I got enough courage to tell the story about the stove, though I cried so much through it I wasn't sure I made any sense. When the entire room had quieted, Father Liam said: "All right. Are there any 'burning desires?' Does anyone have anything they have to say before we close? No? Okay. Everyone stand and join in the Serenity Prayer."

We all stood. I looked at Eddy who motioned for me to pick up my cushion. I followed him to the side of the room. We all made a big circle with our arms on each other. It felt very weird for me to put my arms on so many people so often. Twice in one day. I had never been one for touching, and now it was forced on me. I began to realize, though, that this was not the force of touching that I grew up with. This was gentle and, most importantly, the hands and arms stayed where they should be. Father Liam said: "As we say this prayer tonight, let us remember all the other addicts and alcoholics who are not lucky enough to be in this circle and who are suffering alone."

With that, we all said the prayer. I still had tears in my eyes. Eddy looked at me and said: "Are you okay, man?" I smiled and said: "Yes. I'm fine. Especially since I'm not the one who's still got to clean up."

Primary Cliff

Primary Group was scheduled for an hour three days a week, starting at 10:15 in the morning. It was held in one of the freezing cold therapy rooms, none of which had windows and all of which had glaring artificial lights in the hanging ceiling. With the lights on, the room was not comforting. With the lights on, it was like an examination room, one in which doctors gave physicals or police took statements. When the lights were on, shadows were not allowed.

The patients dressed casually, wearing shorts and pullovers, jeans and T-shirts. The male staff members all wore long sleeved shirts with ties and dress slacks. The women all wore long dresses or business suits.

For my first day, which was my first Monday, I got to the room early, partly out of habit, partly because I knew of nowhere else to go, and partly because I didn't yet realize you could walk the circumference of the entire building in less than a minute. I was worried that I might be late. The door was on the extreme right-hand side of the room as you were looking at it from the entrance. I sat in the third chair on the right-hand side. No one else was in the room yet. I opened my notebook and looked at the schedule to make sure I was in the right place. Traci, the case manager, had outlined in yellow on a master schedule where I was to be. So I was there. I looked at some of the written material in the notebook about something called a "First Step," but none of it made sense.

A short black guy with a very definite sense of purpose and

belonging came in the room. He nodded at me and then sat directly across from me. I smiled at him, but he didn't smile back, though he looked directly at me. He said nothing and neither did I. Other people started coming in and sat down. All of them were men of various ages. The youngest looked like he was fourteen and the oldest looked like he was seventy. Some of them spoke with each other in kidding tones: "Cliff is going to get you...." "Did you get your third step done yet?" "Cliff really slammed that guy." Brand wasn't there and I didn't know anyone else.

The other guys kept talking. At 10:15 exactly in walked Cliff, the man with the Hitler moustache I had seen in the hallway last Friday lecturing Brand. He sat right next to me. He had a metal clipboard with a bunch of papers underneath the clip. On top of the clip was a yellow pen. He passed the clipboard to the guy sitting on his other side and said: "okay. Let's sign in and do a check-in. Who's up?" He was so unlike the way he was on Friday. He was relaxed, nearly cavalier. No one said anything. He put a look on his face not unlike Howdy Doody. "Ah, c'mon," he said. "Do I have to choose someone? You guys know I hate it when you make me act like the counselor. One of you take the lead."

Tom, the guy from the process group last week, said: "Uh, I might as well go." Cliff immediately said: "No, Tom, we're not going to let you go. And you can't go 'til we say so." Tom blushed, crossed his legs together at the thigh, turned sideways towards his left and said in a pleading tone of voice: "Cliff. Don't keep reminding me. I know I can't leave until I get your approval." "Tom," Cliff said, "It's not my approval you should want. It's you getting healthy that you should want. My approval comes after you getting healthy. Not before. So do your check-in."

Tom said: "Well, I've been talking with my wife." Cliff interrupted: "That's good, as opposed to that yelling I heard last week during family conference. What was that all about?" Cliff emphasized the word "that" as though it had forty letter "As" in it and was ended with a capital "T." "You were arguing about you wearing her dress?" Tom answered: "Well, it's just for Halloween." He got this very animated, excited and joyful look on his face. "Every year I get dressed up in a costume with the kids and go trick or treating with them. Before I came, we had planned on me dressing up as Cinderella. That's all." Cliff gave him a look of doubt. "That's all? Y'all got into such a huge fight just over that? It sounded more serious to me. Like she was used to you wearing dresses and was pissed about it." Tom said: "No, Cliff, no," with forced assurance and confidence, as though the manner in which he said "no" would make something true. "She just doesn't want me to sleep with her when I'm home." Cliff interrupted again. "Well, I can see how she might find it confusing, you know, with you wearing her clothes and all. Y'all do what you want to do, but it sounds like she wants some rules." "No," Tom said, "she just doesn't want me there." "Well, hell," Cliff said, "I probably wouldn't either if you were wearing my clothes all the time. Do you stop at underwear? I sure wouldn't want you wearing my underwear." Tom blushed again. Without saying anything, he was giving credence to Cliff's sarcastic assumptions. "C'mon, Cliff," he said, as though he were begging the school bully not to pick on him, while loving the attention at the same time.

Cliff raised his left eyebrow and said: "Okay, let's move along."

Next was a guy who looked fourteen. He was slouched in his

chair, his head aimed at the ceiling, his mouth open. He said nothing. Cliff said: "Someone kick Marty's feet please." Tom did that with glee, giggling as he did. The young guy sat up with a very surprised look on his face. He actually whined and rubbed his eyes with his fists, just like a cartoon or child movie actor would do. "Man, Cliff, I hate coming to your groups. They're too early." Cliff said: "Marty, unlike Tom, you can leave anytime you want. In fact, I can't even remember what's keeping you here." Marty started to smile a smart ass smile, with his lips on one side being raised, showing teeth, while the lower side of the lips were tightly squeezed together. "Oh, yah," said Cliff, "I know why you stay. Because you can't get any money from the family trust fund until we say you're over your various addictions, none of which you think you even have. Did you think about any of this over the weekend at all?" "Well," Marty said as he sat forward in his chair. Then he said nothing. He took a breath like he was going to say something but he just giggled. He looked at Tom, who giggled back. They both blushed and looked down at the floor at the same time. Cliff said: "okay. I see you're having a communicable religious experience, so I'll move along."

The next guy was about forty-five. He was thin and blond with eyes that were nearly pale. He smirked and said: "Well, Cliff, I'm a little pissed. Actually, I'm more than a little pissed." As he spoke, very little of his mouth opened, but it was enough to show very long and yellow teeth. He looked like a white vampire. Cliff said nothing. He simply sat there. The only part of his body which moved were his feet. He took his right foot out of his shoe by placing the toe of the left shoe on the heel of the right. The shoes were common and not quite expensive, cordovan wing tip loafers, the sort of shoe no one under the age of sixty with taste would buy, let alone wear. They had tassels. They were the kind of shoes that were in the closet of a dead grandfather, who, when alive, wore them thinking they were youthful. Cliff's socks were thin-ribbed nylon. They were probably dark blue when not on, but they stretched so thin when on his foot that the blue got this wavy look with each rib a slightly different shade of blue. At the ankle on either side was a pattern. I was too far away, and my eyes were too bad, to see what the pattern was, but it looked like a clock or a compass sign.

Neither one said anything. The clipboard continued to move from person to person. It got to me and I signed my name. I held on to it, unsure if I should pass it on or wait for the silence to end.

None of us were moving. The patient hadn't said his name yet so I called him the Vampire to myself. He leaned back and said in a whining and nasal voice. "C'mon Cliff. Bringing me back on campus was stupid and unfair. I was doing valuable work at my MI site. I did not relapse. I'm as chemically pure as I've ever been." Cliff said: "And that's not a lot, is it?" The Vampire said: "You just don't let up, do you? You just can't let anything go." Cliff quit playing with his shoes, which were worn with the marks of his habit. "No, I can't," he said, "not when your life is on the line. Geoff, you have a disease which wants to kill you. There is no medicine to take to stop it. You can't stop it. You can only control it. This is a serious business. My job is to save your life, even if you don't want me to.

So the Vampire had a name, even a normal one. But I was confused again. I didn't know what "on campus" or "MI site" meant. I also wondered what disease he had. He looked sick. I wondered if he had AIDS, or cancer, or hepatitis. Geoff slouched in his chair and laid his legs out in front of himself. He didn't act angry anymore. Instead, he looked like he was bored. In his whiny voice he said: "okay, Cliff. Whatever you say. You're the expert. You know it all. I'll just sit here until you tell me to move." Cliff said: "That could be a long time. You know, maybe you think you're used to death because you're a funeral director. But you're not immune. I think the formaldehyde you sniffed has pickled your brain." Funeral director? No wonder I thought he looked like a vampire. Sniff formaldehyde? One of my sisters won't even drink instant coffee because it's got formaldehyde in it. Geoff said nothing, but continued to slouch in his chair.

Sitting next to the vampire was a guy who looked like a wrestler. He was about thirty-five or forty. He had a walrus moustache and short dark hair that was cut in a bowl cut. It was easy imagining him looking like a monk. He said: "I'm Mark. I feel -- well today, I feel settled. Not glad, not sad. Just comfortable. I feel right today." Cliff said: "Did your wife tell you to say that?" Mark looked surprised, then laughed and said: "No, Cliff." Cliff was looking around for the clipboard and said: "I'm glad. You're making some progress. Whoever has the clip board, please pass it to me."

Cliff looked at me. I handed him the clipboard which he pulled close to his chest. He started writing on it. "Who are you?" he said. "I'm Ron. This is my first day in here." Cliff said: "I know that, though the rest of the guys in here may not." Then his voiced changed and become softer and comforting. "How y'all doing?" he asked. I felt a jolt. He sounded like he really cared how I was doing. I automatically put on my charm smile but gave a real answer: "I'm confused. I don't understand what these phrases are and it's taking everything I've got just to sit here." Cliff stopped writing, looked directly at me and said: "That's good. If you were comfortable or relaxed, there really would be something wrong with you. After all, you are all in a state licensed mental hospital. From what I hear, you're not here for no reason." What did that mean? What did he know about me? I was getting scared, a status my face must have given away. "Hey!" he said, still looking directly at me. "Are you mad, sad, glad or afraid?" I froze. It wasn't right to be mad. Nobody ever liked it when I was mad. I wasn't sure if I were sad. I was sort of glad I was there and not in jail. And I was definitely afraid. But I couldn't say that. Even though I made my living talking, I couldn't speak. Cliff said: "What are you doing, say, about 1:30?" I reached to my notebook, which I later learned was one of the true giveaway signs of the new patient. "I don't know. Let me look." The short black guy said: "Cliff, he's new. He'll be in lecture." Cliff said: "Yeah, well you can't skip that. Come to my office about 3:30. We'll talk. You finished your psycho-social yet?" "Yes," I said, eager to have something to offer. He said: "Let me have it, then." I said: "I thought I was supposed to give it to Traci." I was getting nervous. I didn't want to upset her. Cliff said: "It's okay. I'm the person she gives it to. While you're here, I'm your treatment dictator. Relax. It can only get better." I didn't say anything. I didn't want to imagine anything worse.

Cliff then looked at Marvin, who took up on the cue and said: "I'm Marvin, a grateful recovering addict child of God." There were audible groans from the other guys. Tom started snickering. Marvin shrugged in a studied and artificial way, which gave away the insincerity of the shrug. "I don't care what you say. I am a child of God and he has removed my cravings and addiction." Cliff leaned back in his chair and started playing with his shoe again. I wasn't sure if those were signs of danger, but I remembered them in order to categorize them for later interpretation and use. "That's good," said Cliff. "It's always good to have a direct relationship with your Higher Power." "Well, then," said Marvin, "why won't you clear me to go to an Afro-American church? I was told by my process group therapist that you have vetoed my request to do that." Cliff said: "The entire treatment team vetoed it based upon my recommendation." Marvin leaned forward and put his hands together as though he were going to pray. His hands were huge, greatly oversized for his body. They looked like they belonged on the hands of a giant. He asked with great deliberation and calmness: "Why?" The deliberate calmness seemed as false and studied as the shrug. Cliff said: "Why do you think?" Marvin said: "To be honest...." Cliff interrupted: "That would a nice change." Marvin looked a little pissed for just a second, then smiled as though Cliff's sarcasm was meaningless, as though Cliff was a child talking to an adult. Marvin held his hands, still together, up in the air and looked at the ceiling as he said: "Let me continue." His voice was louder. Even though there was no noise in the room, he acted and sounded like he was a put-upon parent trying to talk over a loud stereo to his teenager. "I think there's only one reason. You're not going to like it, but you're a southern boy and you don't even recognize it. I think you're a racist."

Cliff stopped playing with his shoe. Now I realized that not playing with the shoe meant that he was serious and concentrating. Maybe when he played with his shoe was when he was open to, and collecting, all information. Cliff said: "Marvin, you've set yourself up to believe that. There is nothing I can say or do to change your belief except to give in to it, which I'm not going to do. You know the rules. You can go to church, but you have to have two other guys go with you. You haven't asked anyone to go. Get two other guys and you can go to any church you want." Marvin moved his head down and his hands apart in another studied move: this one of supplication. "Cliff, there are no other black patients right now and no white guy is going to go to a black church." Besides his words, his tone of voice said: "Are you crazy? This is simple. This is the real meaning of the purpose of the universe." Cliff said: "Do you know? Have you asked?" Geoff said in a lazy voice, "Hell, I'll go with you. Anything to get off campus." Cliff immediately said, and without looking at him, "That's why you can't go, Geoff." Marvin said: "See? Even when someone will go you won't let them." Cliff said: "You didn't ask him. You didn't ask for help. His volunteering doesn't count. It's your lesson to learn, not his. You can't expect people to read your mind and come to you. That's the problem with all addicts: they think they should get their own way by just existing."

That floored me. I thought about myself and how I expected other people to know what I wanted, to behave the way I wanted without me saying a word, and then how I got angry when they didn't do what I expected. Cliff said: "Ask the guys in this room. If you can get two, you can go." Marvin sat back in his chair, put a smile on his face that the Buddha would have envied except for its insincerity and said: "You're not letting me go." Cliff said: "We've been through this many times. You're not letting me go." There was a silence in the room. Even Tom had stopped snickering and he was looking at his feet. Then Cliff said to

Marvin: "How do you feel?" There was a longer silence. Marvin went through many looks on his face with the speed of light until he settled on one of resignation, then he said: "I'm angry but accepting. I have to learn to accept all kinds of asinine things. But as a child of God, I can do that." Each time he said: "child of God," it came across as an important title, as though it was emblazoned "CHILD OF GOD" on his forehead.

Cliff waited a moment and then he said: "I'm not going to argue with you. But think about this. Do you know Betty?" Marvin said, with disgust in his voice, "Oh, yeah, we all know Betty, 'The Lesbian From The University Of Chicago.' It's her self-made title. That's how she introduces herself all the time. And," apparently quoting her, 'the only reason she's here is because the University of Chicago sent her and because she's an open and avowed lesbian.'" "Right," Cliff said questioningly, "And you've already figured out that there's more to her than her profession, where she works and her sexuality." Marvin simply said: "Yeah," knowing where this was going and not liking it. "See," Cliff said, "she sets herself up for rejection and failure. She lives in an impossibility box. All her difficulties, hardships and rejections come from that. She won't listen to anything else. The problem is not hers, it's the worlds. As long as she believes that the world is made to satisfy her, she'll never get out of that box." Marvin said, "So, you're saying I'm the same way?" Cliff said: "What do you think?" Marvin acted for real as he said: "But Cliff, she is a lesbian! She's damned. God will never accept her." Cliff quietly said: "It wasn't that long ago society said the same thing about blacks." Marvin looked as though he had been slapped. His jaw clenched. He clenched his hands into fists, opened his mouth but said nothing. He sat back and said: "I'm still a child of God."

Cliff said: "Let me know when everyone is, will 'ya?"

First Interview of Cliff

I went to Cliff's office which was across the hall from the therapy rooms. I stood there not knowing what to do. The door was closed and I didn't know if I should knock. Another patient went by and said: "Are you waiting for Cliff?" I said: "Yes." The patient said: "He's notorious for being late. Of course, he could just be in there playing games on his computer. So knock." I smiled and said: "Uh, I'm sort of afraid." The patient laughed and said: "Yeah, I can understand that. Okay, then just stand there. Maybe something will happen."

No one else was in the hall. I waited about five minutes and then approached the door. I stood in front of it getting up the courage to knock. Just as I got close enough, the door opened inward and another counselor, a very short man, came out. He obviously wasn't expecting anyone so close to the door and he walked into me. "Oh, sorry," he said. "Are you waiting for Cliff?" "Yes," I said, wondering how he knew. "He'll be right here. Just get comfortable and wait."

Wait? Where? So I sat in the hallway like I was a student. I opened my notebook and placed it across my legs. I started to read the pages about the First Step. They were incomprehensible but I tried to make some sense of them. I put my elbows on my thighs and my head in my hands. I think I started to sleep because I was not aware of Cliff coming up to me. He startled me and said: "One of us is late, and I'm the boss so it's not me. I wonder who it is?" I looked up at him and said: "It's the guy who just left."

As I stood up he walked into his office, I followed him. He put down his clipboard and picked up another. I stood there, expecting him to tell me where to sit. He looked at some papers on his desk and said: "We won't do it in here. I share the office and there will be too many interruptions. Let's go across the hall to my other office." I backed up and followed him out of his office and across the hall into a therapy room.

"I thought you said this was your other office?" I said. He replied, "It is as long as I'm in here." He closed the door. I asked: "Won't someone come in here?" He said: "Not as long as I'm in here." He sat down in a chair and pulled another chair close enough to use as an ottoman. He kicked the heels of both shoes loose, put them on the other chair and crossed his legs at the ankles. I sat in a chair to the side of him.

"I've read your questionnaire, but I want to just talk with you before we discuss it." He put his clipboard on his lap and turned over the top page of the pad which was on it. He drew a big circle in the center. Then he said: "Both parents alive?" I said: "No. My dad died three years ago last July." "What of?" he asked. "Being mean,' I said. He arched his eyes and looked at me. "Congestive heart failure," I amended. "How old?" he wanted to know. "Seventy-nine years, I think. There was some problem with his birth certificate so he might have been eighty. His parents were immigrants from Hungary and we've been told that they didn't even register a birth until the child was a year old because so many died in the first year."

"What about your mother?" he said. "What about her?" I asked back. "She's still alive. Plays golf two or three days a week. She's seventy-eight and in pretty good health."

As I spoke, he drew lines out from the center circle and made little circles at the end of them. He wrote something in the circles I couldn't read. "What about your siblings?" I said: "I suppose I shouldn't say what about them again, should I?" He didn't say anything. I said: "I've got two brother and two sisters. The oldest is Bonnie, who is ten years older than I am. Her health is okay, as far as I know. Everyone's in pretty good health, though we've all had our share of accidents. The next is Beverly." "Whoa, hold on," he said, "Don't just tell me their names. Tell me about them."

"Okay," I said. "Bonnie has been married twice. She had five kids from her first marriage. She got divorced and later married her high school sweetheart. She and her husband are retired." He was drawing more lines and circles, not looking at me. "Beverly lost her husband, Craig, to pancreatic cancer two years ago." "Ouch," he said. "Ouch," I asked. "That's a painful way to go," he replied. "Yeah," I said. "It was horrible. He and I were very close. Anyway, they have two children, both grown and on their own." He drew another line and circle. "Next is Bob who is married to Nancy. She's a wonderful person." "And Bob isn't?" he asked. "No," I said, "Bob is okay, but Nancy is like a saint. They have two kids, both of whom work for me. The elder is in college and the younger is in high school. They're great, too." He kept drawing lines and making circles. "Then there is Rick. He's married with two daughters, both still in elementary school." "Are you close to him?" he asked. "I was growing up, but he lives in another city, and we don't really see much of each other. But, yeah, I feel close to him. I feel sorry for him too. He just got a diagnosis of cancer. We don't know what it is yet or how serious." Cliff drew more lines and more circles. "Hold on just a second," he said.

"Describe your relationship with your parents," he said. "Hmm. Well, my dad was either Satan or Santa. He was either great or horrible, depending upon how much he had to drink. My mother...." "Stop," he said. "Did you love your father?" "Love? What do you mean 'love?' Yeah, I guess I did." I took a long pause and Cliff looked at me. I said: "I'm not sure what you mean." He said: "It's sort of like that old saying: 'if you've got to ask what it costs, you can't afford it. If you've got to define it, you probably don't have it."

I listened and said nothing. This was getting painful. I could get up and leave if I wanted, but I liked his attention and, to be honest, I was desperate for any personal attention, even if I had to pay money for it and suffer emotionally for it.

Cliff said: "What about your mother?" I said, "What about her? She's had a hard life: Two marriages, five children, an alcoholic, violent and promiscuous husband. Children who are accomplished on the outside, and screwed up on the inside." Cliff said: "You're sounding like a storyteller. Don't tell me your mother's story. Tell me how you felt about her." I couldn't say anything. I was so tempted to be the reporter or the lawyer, telling a story or advocating a point of view. He looked at me directly. His eyes were so brown, so deep, and they appeared so kind. I said: "I felt..." then I stopped. Feelings were not something I was taught to express. They were to be handled, dealt with, and put aside as I went on to some undefined something, some place where they would not matter because they would be perfect. Cliff just continued to look at me. I started to separate again and looked at us as though I were a camera, floating above us. He must have noticed something because he said: "Hey, hey, hey. What's going on? Where are you?" Was it that obvious that I wasn't there? I don't know. I can't read my own face unless I'm floating above it. I said: "I simply felt that she never loved me; that I was a burden to her. Objectively speaking, I was a burden." Cliff said nothing and wrote nothing. I started to cry silently. I didn't move but stared at the ceiling wanting to tell him how horrible I felt, how miserable I had been. He said: "Don't you feel that anyone has loved you?" I drew a breath, feeling ridiculous that at my age, that I should be acting like this. Then I sobbed: "Yes. My brother-in-law who died. He is the only person who ever loved me for me, myself, without a sense of obligation or duty." "Hmmm," Cliff said, "that's deep analytical despair. What about your sister who brought you here?" I said, "Objectively speaking, yes, of course she loves me, but I expect everyone to tell me they never did. I am always ready to be pushed away. I always prepare for it." "And in the preparation," Cliff said, "you tend to make sure it happens by not connecting, is that right?"

Dr. Handle

Once a day for a week, all new patients were required to attend a special lecture series on the science and society of addiction. This was held in a conference room with a huge table around which we all sat in executive style swivel chairs. The lectures were very popular and patients who were scheduled for discharge came back to listen to, but not participate in, the lectures before they went home.

The lecturer was Dr. Handle, a very short, elderly looking man, who interjected his lectures with stories of addiction that could only be comprehended by another addict. He always wore a red tie or scarf around his neck, as though he were a stylized, pompous and typecast director of serious theatre. Dr. Handle required us to disclose our stories in the group, then he'd ask us to come up with an explanation as to why we did what we did. When we couldn't, which was often, he gave us his answer.

On the first day I was there, Dr. Handle looked at this young, very handsome, white male surgeon and said: "Tell us why you think you're here."

The surgeon told us that he had been getting high using whatever he could scam off his patients. He'd write prescriptions for powerful pain medications a patient didn't need. He'd keep the patients on the pain medications longer than was needed or was healthy. He told us that most surgeons never get to know their patients, but that he made house calls after the surgery, which created his great popularity among his patients. While in their homes, he'd raid their medicine cabinets for a small portion of the pain pills. As his addiction got worse, the small portions increased until finally a patient or two put two and two together. His partners were called and then so were the police. Even after the initial investigation, he kept doing it until he was arrested.

After the arrest, he continued to practice, but he was placed under close supervision. The supervision worked concerning his prescription manipulation. He stopped stealing them. He kept making his house calls but took a few detours between homes to go to crack houses where he started buying crack. Once he left the operating room during patient preparation to go to a crack house, still wearing his surgical greens. When he came back he was unable to operate, which apparently was obvious to everyone but the patient, who died as a result of the doctor's manipulations, not having the same tolerance to the crack that the doctor did. He was suspended and went into detox for seven days. He came out smiling that he was cured. He was so charming that no one doubted the cure took, but his wife was still a little nervous.

His wife worked and, since he was suspended, he didn't. While she worked, his wife left their newborn child in his care. Every morning, before she left, they'd have coffee together. He was trying to charm and please her, so he took to baking fresh rolls or muffins in their newly installed, professional kitchen which had eight gas burners, just in case they decided to throw some huge parties or have a small intimate dinner with an extraordinary amount of hot sauces.

While sipping the coffee, they'd eat the hot pastries, which were made with love, and she'd quiz him like she was the CIA. She lectured him on care and trust as though she were an evangelist. He always smiled at her, and he had the cutest and most endearing way of tearing his pastry apart in tiny, bite-size pieces.   Sometimes, he'd get her giggling and he'd feed her the tiny, love-touched pieces. He promised he'd be good. He promised he'd be right by the telephone. He'd even clean the house. Why not? It would save a few bucks.

She went to work. This went on for a few weeks. When she got home, she sometimes thought he was acting a little more loose than normal, but he assured her his looseness was due to the exorcism of the drug devil. Still, she checked up on him by calling him often and at irregular times.

Unknown to her, and why would she think of it anyway, he put call forwarding on their home telephone and had all calls transferred to his state-of-the-art mobile telephone. As soon as she left for work, he'd feed the baby a small portion of an over-the-counter antihistamine so the child would yawn and sleep very soundly. Then he'd drink the last of the coffee and leave the house in his big black, solid, and very quiet Mercedes to go to a seedy liquor store to score some crack and some vodka to wash it down.

He made sure that he timed himself exactly never to be gone longer than ten minutes. It took his wife twenty minutes to get home from work so he thought that if he were gone for only ten, then he would always beat her home. If she called, which she did, the wonderful and reassuring quiet of the solid Mercedes interior would disguise his location. Even if the phone rang when he was in the liquor store, he could run back into his car, make sure the windows were up and tell his wife just how great he was. "The baby?" he'd say, "Oh, she's sleeping." This went on for a while. Everyone seemed safe. The schedule never varied. He always beat her home. But one day someone else got there first.

On the first minute of his ten-minute trip that day, when he was just out of the neighborhood, an electrical fire started. Apparently the coffee pot just got too hot. On the second minute of that ten minute trip, his wife called. He pulled over. She was at work. He could tell for sure because of the background noise. On the third minute of that ten-minute trip, the small electrical fire decided to grow up. On the fourth minute, he pulled into the liquor store and said with a big charming smile to the clerk: "Just my regular, please," causing the clerk to smile as though they both had the best private joke in the world. On the fifth minute, the gas burner professional stove, which he had forgotten to turn off, reached a point where it couldn't help but attract the attention of the fire. On the sixth minute, his house blew up and his baby died. On the ninth minute he arrived home to be greeted by the first of many fire engines. When he pulled into his lovely neighborhood it took him a few minutes to figure out what was going on. He was pretty high, and the flames held his attention, unlike his burning house, his baby, and his former life.

He told us this story in this same summary manner, as though he were reading a police report written by a literate cop. He stopped talking. He had no expression on his face. No one said anything. The shock of the story knocked us as flat as the explosion did his house. Dr. Handle stood there, saying nothing, but he threw a piece of chalk up in the air and then caught it as it came down again. He kept doing this: chalk up, chalk down, catch. Chalk up, chalk down, catch.

He didn't look at the surgeon, but looked at us as a group and said: "Anyone know why this happened?" There was no response. He waited a minute: chalk up, chalk down, catch. Then he looked at Billy, who was sitting next to me and asked him directly. "What did you do for a living?" Billy said, "I'm a doctor." Dr. Handle gave this thin, tight little smile and said: "You speak in the present tense. Oh, well, we'll leave your delusions for another day. Ever do crack?" Billy said: "No." Dr. Handle said: "What was your drug of choice?" Billy said: "Mostly downers." Dr. Handle nodded understandingly, as though this were the most normal thing and said: "How many would you take a day?" Billy said: "Sixty to a hundred, depending upon the day." Dr. Handle smiled more broadly as though he had just diagnosed the hardest case. He started tossing the chalk again. Up, down, catch. Up, down, catch. "Yep," he said, "You're an addict."

"Okay," he continued, "Let's put the first question aside for a minute and ask a new one. Why didn't our charming, handsome surgeon commit suicide? Think about it. He's been arrested for drug violations, a patient dies on the operating table, he violates the trust of his wife; his house explodes and his baby dies. I assume his wife has left him and filed for divorce." Dr. Handle looked at the doctor and asked, "She has, hasn't she?" The doctor didn't say anything. He had no expression on his face, and simply nodded his head up and down.

Dr. Handle said: "Okay, we now have two questions on the table. They're really the same question, but let's keep them split to make it easier for you. Why did this happen is the first one. The second one is why didn't this wonderful doctor commit suicide?" He looked at the doctor and asked: "Are you on suicide watch?" The doctor looked down and said "No," as though not being on suicide watch were a shameful thing. Dr. Handle looked in my direction, pointed a piece of chalk at me and said: "But you're on suicide watch, right?" I froze, but said: "Yes."

Dr. Handle then said: "Did you kill anyone?" "No," I said. He said: "You're a lawyer, right?" Again I said "Yes." "So," he said, "no patients died under your watch. But did you ever blow a case by being drunk?" "No," I said. "But," he said, "You got arrested, too, right?" "Yes," I said. He gave me a kindly smile and said: "I won't embarrass you too much right now, but you got arrested for trying to get the wrong guy in bed with you; right?" I was mortified by his use of the word "guy." I hadn't told any of the patients what my arrest was about, but I said: "Yes."

He smiled again and said: "Looking for love in all the wrong places?" I was getting very upset. Great drops of sweat were dripping down my sides. I said, "That's a good way of putting it."   He turned away from me, tossing and catching his chalk again. "C'mon, people, think!" No one said anything.

"Okay, because it's the first day I'll help you. The doctor's misery happened because he's an addict. He didn't commit suicide because he's an addict, and his disease, which wants him dead, figures he's still a good host. Our attorney friend here is on suicide watch because his disease figures he's not a good host and wants him dead now. Remember this: you have a disease. All diseases have the same goal: kill the host. It's that simple."

He put both of his hands on the top of the table, palms flat, and leaned forward. "Listen people. You all think you are kings and queens of the world. You think the rules don't apply to you, that they are there for your amusement. All chemically dependent people share a number of qualities and rule-breaking is one of the most common. You are king and queen babies. You are children at the same time you think you are the rulers of the universe. You hold your pain inside so deep and are so afraid to touch it."

He looked at the surgeon. "Look at him. He told you the most horrific story and with a few exceptions you just sat there. Don't you think his experiences were painful? Yet he told the story as though he were reading a lawyer's summary. Those of you who cried, continue to cry. Tears mean you're finally connecting with some feelings." I thought to myself: well, if the tears are such a good sign, why am I feeling so miserable?

Dr. Handle went on: "You all live in the past or the future. None of you live in the now. You avoid the present for any number of reasons, but mostly because you can't control it, and every single one of you is a control freak. You can control your past because you can control your memory. You can control the future because it's a fantasy creation. You avoid the present." He was still leaning on the table, but he lifted his palms and slapped them loudly on the table top: "Be here now!" he shouted. We were all startled.

"Listen: you are chemically dependent because you were born with a gene that said you could be. At some point in the past of each of you there was a traumatic event or a series of events which triggered that gene and it became active. You used a defense of personality like withdrawal, or humor, or isolation to defend against that trauma. A person who isn't an addict uses a defense only when necessary and then they stop using it. We addicts use it over and over again and it then becomes our personality."

"How many of you," he asked, "swore you would never become like your parents?" Nearly all of the hands went up. He pointed at a middle-aged woman with thin, blond, wispy hair and asked her: "What quality did your parents have that you promised yourself you'd never have?" She answered: "I promised I'd never be violent." Dr. Handle said: "Why? What was your background like?" She said: "My parents were very violent. My dad was an alcoholic and my mother was a classic enabler. He beat her and us. When he was through beating her and us, then she'd beat us." Dr. Handle grabbed his chalk again but this time just rubbed it between his palms. He looked at the ceiling and said: "Are you married?"

She said: "Yes."

He said: "Do you have children?"

She said: "Yes. Three."

He said: "What did you do for a living?"

She sat up straight in her chair, cleared her throat, and said: "I was, and still am, a doctor."

He smiled, still looking at the ceiling, still rubbing the chalk between his hands and asked: "What does your husband do?"

She said: "He's a doctor too."

Dr. Handle stopped rubbing the chalk, looked directly at her and said: "And what promises did you make to yourself as a child?"

She said: "That I'd never be married to a violent man; that I'd never be violent, and that I'd never hit my children."

He smiled his encouraging smile, put one hand on the table top and rubbed the back of his ear with the chalk. He said: "Were you able to keep the promises?"

She said: "No. My husband and I hit each other and our children."

He asked her: "Where are your children now?"

She answered: "The oldest one ran away; the second one was taken away, and the youngest still lives with us." He smiled, nodding his head again, as though this were the most normal thing in the world. His eyes went to the ceiling again, as though he were seriously thinking about this, then he looked at her again and said: "So, you became the person you promised you'd never be?"

She started to talk, stopped, sat up straighter and said: "Well, yes, I guess so, though I never thought of it that way." He said to her: "Is there another way to think of it?" She said nothing. None of us said anything. He started tossing the chalk up again, not so high, with just one hand. He looked at each of us in the face, tossing the chalk up and down. He repeated himself: "Is there any other way to look at it?"

I looked at him and said: "So you're saying the victim becomes the victimizer." He stopped tossing the chalk and started rubbing it between his hands again. He smiled and said: "Leave it to a lawyer to get to the point. Yes, that's exactly what I'm saying." He looked directly at me and said: "Was your background any different?" I said: "No, not really. Lots of violence and drinking, but my mother was never physically abusive. My dad never hit me, but he sexually abused me when I was in seventh grade."

He gave me his encouraging smile again and I started to sweat. I knew this smile meant trouble. "And here you are, having lived the life of a victim. Ever do any victimizing?"

I didn't know what to say. I sure didn't like the title. But I said: "Yes, I did. To be honest, it seemed normal." He said: "'I thought this was normal' could be the title of a book. We all thought it was normal.

We are what we learn." He looked at me and said: "What's your earliest memory?" I thought for a moment and said: "Christmas when I was two-and-a-half years old. I was outside in the snow with just pants and socks on. My two older brothers were shooting ping-pong balls out of guns at me." He wiped his right hand across his right eye. "Yes," he said, "I remember those. You're a lot older than you look. Maybe we caught you in time. And ever since, you've been the victim; right?" "Well," I said, "I never consciously thought of myself that way." "Maybe not," he said, "but I bet you have a sense of entitlement; right?" I didn't say anything. He continued: "What kind of car do you drive?" I told him: "I have two cars, a Cadillac and a 4-wheel drive." He laughed and said: "And, of course, you drive those at the same time, right?" I was beginning to get what he meant.

"People," he said, "listen. Your trauma and your addiction have turned you into the person you said you'd never be. Look at yourself honestly. If you do, then together we can all help you become the person you should be, the person you were meant to be, the person you want to be. But to do this, you must be rigorously honest with yourselves. You cannot suffer from embarrassment or shyness. You cannot hold back. If you do, if you hold back even in the slightest, then your disease will use that space to hide and rest up. It will get stronger and when it's ready, it will come back with a vengeance. This is a progressive disease. If you stop using and pick up again, it will be like you never quit. If you quit for a year and start again, it will be like you continued to use for that year."

He stopped talking and wiped his forehead with his shirt sleeve. I hadn't noticed it, but he was sweating. "I didn't start using any drugs until I was nearly fifty, but once I started it was like I was a lifetime user. My use was so bad my wife made me undress in front of her as soon as I got home. I had to give her all my clothes and then she'd give me a new set to wear. This included my underwear. So every day I'd come home, strip in the foyer, give her the clothes and put on the new ones. One time I told her I wanted to take a shower because it was so hot. This was in the days before central air conditioning."

"So I went up to my shower, naked. My bathroom had a black and white tile floor. You know those floors? Little black tiles grouted in next to little white ones? I couldn't wait to take a shower. I shut the door, turned the water on and then opened the medicine cabinet to get a jar of Vaseline. Anyone know why I wanted the Vaseline?"

I didn't. All I could think of was some sexual thing. A guy at the end of the table said: "So you could fuck yourself?" We all laughed. Dr. Handle did, too, and said, "Close, but no cigar."

"I had smuggled this glass vial home from the hospital in my ass. It has pure, uncut cocaine in it. I greased up my fingers so I could get it out. I bent over, reached in and slowly and delicately pulled it out. But I was so excited, or maybe I had just used too much Vaseline, that the vial slipped out of my hand and shot across the floor. It hit that wonderful art-deco black and white tile floor and smashed into a million pieces. Does anyone know what I did then?"

The female doctor said: "Clean it up?" The guy who talked about fucking himself said: "You licked it up."

Dr. Handle stood still with a goofy grin on his face. "Yes. I licked it up, glass shards and all. After a while, my tongue was so numb from the cocaine that I didn't feel anything. I got so high that I didn't even notice the pain or the tracks of blood on the floor. I took my shower, got dressed and went downstairs to my wife. She looked at me and said 'Did you cut your lips shaving?' I looked at her and said: 'I wasn't shaving.' She then screamed when she saw my tongue which was lacerated as though I had taken a razor blade to it. That's the power of the disease."

He said nothing for a while. Then he said: "I still get cravings when I talk about drugs. People, our time is nearly up for today, but I want you to remember this. The fact that you have a disease doesn't define your moral character. The way you act defines your moral character. You are not responsible for your disease, but you sure are responsible for your recovery. You all have addictive personalities. You can't get rid of that. It's what makes you great at what you do. But you can get addicted to recovery. Now go. Tomorrow we will talk about the addictive quality of carrots."

Meeting Andy

I saw Andy before I met him. He was lying face down with his head in the curve of one arm while the other was laid out straight above his head, as though he were pointing. One leg was tucked up underneath him and the other was straight back, like a ruler. He looked like he was doing an imitation of Superman, flying, but on the ground behind our apartment building. The ground was half dirt and half unmown clumps of grass. It was just a strip, really, behind the apartments and before the cyclone fence which was topped with barbed wire. Beyond the fence were tall spindly pine trees. Andy's apartment was directly across from mine. We shared an overhang and a concrete walk. There were all kinds of chairs littering the walk and the ground. There were cheap plates with mold on them and coffee cans filled with old cigarette butts under the chairs and against the wall. There was a beaten, scraped and stained wooden coffee table about 2 feet square upon which were more moldy plates and three ashtrays, all full. There was a broken pot with old coke cans and big plastic bottles. There were big black garbage bags and smaller white ones, stacked up against the walls, waiting for someone to take them to the garbage bin. This is where we lived.

Someone spoke to Andy. I thought for sure he must be asleep to lie there like that. It was very hot yet he had on long green Army pants. He had on two shirts; the top one was long sleeved. His hair was thick and yellow, like George Armstrong Custer's was supposed to have been. Only someone, I thought, dead asleep could lie on that ill-defined ground, directly in the sunlight and with all those clothes on. "Hey!" Andy muttered back. I could have sworn he was dead asleep. I still had a lot to learn about drug addicts. "Yeah?" he said, even though no one had responded to him. "What's going on?" A roommate of his said: "This is Ron. He lives across the way. This is Andy." To me, the roommate said: "You'll have to forgive him. He just got here late last night and from what I understand, he's one hell of a drug addict."

Andy stood up, blinked his eyes, opened his mouth and rubbed it with his tongue a few times. He held out his hand, which I took and shook. He said: "How ya' doing?" I said: "okay. Wait. Um, I'm not supposed to say 'Okay' or 'Fine.' Uh, I'm all right but hot. It's cool back home. Aren't you hot with all those clothes on sleeping in the sun?" "No. I'm cold, man. Those apartments are way too cold." I thought he was kidding but one of his roommates, a medical Professor, said: "Andy is addicted to lots of drugs including narcotics and opiates. When you withdraw from those, you get cold and stay cold for a while. I, myself, wore a wool overcoat for a month this summer." The Professor was from France and often spoke very formally. I still thought they were kidding me. We were in Georgia. Any summer month in Georgia is intolerable. This was October and it was still hot. I was very aware that I was new to all this and thought they were kidding me and said so. The Professor said: "No. This is true." He said it with such sincerity and such a look of wonder on his face that I took it for true.

Andy was in his late twenties. The Professor was in his late forties. I was in my forties too, but looked like I was in my twenties and certainly acted younger than that. Andy stood there while we were talking with a grin on his face that confirmed the Professor. His grin was goofy and an invitation to trouble, I could tell. He was real cute, but I kept staring at his face because it seemed like I saw two faces on the same body. I hadn't had anything to drink for about ten days and was off my detox medication, but I still stared, thinking I was hallucinating. How could anyone have two faces simultaneously? Somehow Andy did, but only for that split second it takes the brain to register something. Then the image focused on a cheerful and attractive face. "Hey, man," he said. "You don't play golf, do ya'?" He had this unusual Southern accent. Unlike most southerners, he spoke fast. "I do a little, but I don't keep score, and I don't play with people who lecture about it." He laughed and said: "Cool. We gotta go sometime." The Professor said to me: "You're eating dinner with us." I started to beg off, not knowing what the rules were about joining other apartments. He said, in a more commanding voice, "No, no. You cannot say no. These apartments eat together a lot. I cook. You eat. That's it." So I said: "Thanks. What time?" He smiled and said: "Time does not matter here. After all, where are you going to go? You must stay with us in any event. Talk with Andy while I cook."

Andy acted like he was waking up even though he said he had not been sleeping. He said: "What's going on, man?" I found out later that this was his favorite phrase. He said it instead of thinking. He said it like he was a machine, warming up, humming up, making sounds. He said it in the same manner, and with as much sincerity, as a politician when he says: "Thanks for your vote." "Not much," I said. "Are you really that cold?" "Hmm. Uh, yeah. I've been through this before. It'll last a few weeks. But they gave me some medication to help me get through it." "Before?" I asked. I had a hard time believing anyone could go through this more than once. It was supposed to take on the first time. It was already way too painful to do more than once. I said that to Andy, who grinned and said: "Yeah. I just came here from a place in Louisiana. Actually, they kicked me out, because I kept paying a kid to smuggle me in cocaine." I thought he was kidding. Who would go into a rehabilitation center, which was nearly locked-down, with people around you constantly to get you better, and use drugs during treatment? I asked him this. He just laughed and said: "Most everyone, that's who."

I couldn't accept or reject his statement. I told myself to ask my roommate, Eddy, about it later. Eddy had been a professional drug counselor. He also said he had been in over fifty rehab programs and jails. He was a very well educated man. He tried to jump off the Mackinac Bridge but was talked down. That is the bridge between the two peninsulas of Michigan where Lake Michigan meets Lake Huron. It can be dangerous just driving across it. One time, and not so long ago, the wind picked up a car and threw it off the bridge, driver and all. The car, with the driver, fell hundreds of feet where it immediately sank. People thought about trying to save the driver, but she was dead as soon as the wind decided to sneeze. The authorities had to wait months for the water to get calm enough to send professional divers down to find the car. When they did, the driver looked as though nothing had happened to her. The water there is so cold that it will keep packaged lunch meat fresh for seventy years. Except for the part about talking to Eddy, I told all this to Andy.

"Cool, man. Wow! What do you think went through her head when she flipped over the edge?"

"I don't know. Probably nothing except confusion. It would have happened so fast."

"Do you think she was alive when she hit the water?"

"I don't know. I hope not."

"You know, they could dissect her and tell. You can tell when you cut the body, check the lungs...." That was the word he used: dissect. I said: "Hey. If I wanted to know this stuff, I would have been a doctor." Andy grinned. "Sorry, man." Someone must have already told him I was a lawyer. I said: "What do you do?" Andy smiled and said: "Did. No do. I am an addict. I used to be a medical researcher doing pharmacological research on drugs. I've been trying for eight years to get into the same medical school." Thinking I may have misheard him, I said: "Did you only apply to the one?" He said: "Yeah." I said: "There are lots of medical schools." He interrupted me with a look of violent anger on his face, which was now bright red. His green eyes were nearly invisible he had clenched his face so tight. "Those fuckers have no right to reject me! They're stupid and I'm not." I looked at him and said: "Are they addicts too?" He looked like he wanted to hit me, but grabbed his breath, let it out, smiled and said: "No. They're not. But they're still stupid."

The Professor hollered at another guy to start the grill. He came to us and said: "The coals must be just right - perfect - and then we can grill the salmon; yes? I would cook beef, but you cannot get good beef here like you can in the North or in South America. These southerners know pork and chicken but they do not know beef. So we must content ourselves with salmon, which comes in fresh every day." Andy and I looked at each other. I wasn't sure if the Professor was joking so I said: "You would have loved my father. He was also very grill conscious," to which the Professor looked at me with wide eyes and said: "Ah, yes.

Was he French?" I said: "No. He was Hungarian." The Professor's eyes widened further and he said: "Ah, the Hungarians know food second only to the French. Actually better sometimes. Can you cook?" Without waiting for my answer he said: "Of course you can. You must cook for us sometime."

Andy looked at me and I at him, both of us smiling. He said: "You've got to understand. The Professor used to make his own drugs. He had his own secret lab. He probably never would have been caught but that he was giving experimental medication to patients." I looked at the Professor and said: "Is that right?" He said: "Yes, of course. The government did not care about their suffering. I did." Then he laughed just as Andy started laughing and talking at the same time: "Well, of course, he had to take his own medication just to make sure it really did stop pain." The Professor said: "Ah. If only I would have had Andy to try my drugs. But, you must understand, what I had a whole lab to do, Andy did with a coffee maker and a hot plate."

Andy just laughed. To this day he is the only person I know who can laugh and talk at the same time. He said: "And I wouldn't have been caught except for the smell. I didn't have strong enough fans." The guy starting the fire said: "Yeah, and kicking the cop didn't help either." Andy's face changed again as he said: "Well, she shouldn't have been pretending she was straight. Everyone knows she was a dyke so why was she mad when I shouted it? I don't care if she's queer, I just think all cops should be honest."

This statement got me scared because I was gay and had not been honest about it until I got into treatment. Even then, I was not being emotionally honest. I had told the other guys with whom we lived what was going on, but Andy was new. I didn't know if anyone had spoken to him or what. I was afraid to say anything, not knowing what the reaction would be. Everyone was silent for a minute and then I said: "Queer is a word no one should use, Andy. It's putting someone down in a pretty harsh way." Andy got this knowing grin on his face and said: "You gotta understand, really, some of my best friends are queer...er...gay. The guy I did most of my drugs with was so gay, I think he was a new species. But, hell, could he kick out and party! I used to go to gay dance clubs with him. I'd just be dressed in a leather vest and shorts. Man, did I get some attention and great drugs."

I was getting both very interested and very uncomfortable. I didn't know where the conversation was going. The Professor had gone back into the apartment. So I said: "What did you do with the attention?" Andy said: "Nothing, really I truly like women when it comes to sex, but when it comes to partying, there is nothing better than a fucked up gay man with AIDS. He's got all kinds of drugs he wants to share and he welcomes a dramatic death." I didn't know what to make of this conversation. The Professor came back out and said: "Hey, Ron! Can you make a salad?" I said: "Yes. With homemade croutons and dressing." He said, "Well, then, do it. If you can make a salad, we will let you cook community meal on Wednesday."

I went back into my apartment where it seemed like a cold dark cave. I was so glad to be out of the heat. I was also real glad to have something to do while I thought about the talk of drugs and sex. Even though I wasn't supposed to be left alone, I was for a few minutes. Then Andy walked into the apartment without knocking. "Hey!" he said. I was startled, and he told me that "No one knocks. Everyone treats all the apartments and stuff in them like it's their own. Sort'a communistic if you ask me. I really don't care what ya' touch, just don't touch my golf clubs."

A Florid Tapestry

Once a day at 9:15 a.m. on the dot, all the patients assembled in the all-purpose room. The chairs were lined up against three walls. The chairs on the fourth wall were brought towards the center of the room. They were placed in a nearly even row, with the center chair of that row pushed forward a few inches. In that chair sat the patient who was, over the next hour, going to deliver his or her first step. Straight across from that person was the wall clock. It was large, like a clock in an elementary school. It had a red sweep second hand. Each minute was marked off. Even someone with poor eyesight could see that red second hand.

The deliverer sat with the members of his or her dome. On the right hand sat a person to whom the deliverer felt close. It was this person's job to take each page of the notes from which the deliverer read, as that page was read, in as unobtrusive manner as possible. This sounds simple, but within five minutes of starting, the deliverer was coughing, crying, sobbing, bending over, swaying or catatonic. The right-handed person's job was to nudge, prod, wink at, blink at or whisper at the deliverer to keep that person going. Again, this was to be done in a manner as unobtrusive as possible. It was the deliverer's day to feel. The right-hand was only there to assist in the maintenance of the first step itself so that the deliverer could feel.

The creation and presentation of the first step was very structured. The first step itself is based upon the "steps" in the Alcoholics Anonymous book. There are twelve of them. The first one says: "We admitted we were powerless over alcohol—that our lives had become unmanageable." We were give written instructions on how to write it. There were classes we had to attend to help us present it. There were categories that had to be answered. "Give five examples of each of the following: 1) how your disease impacted the feelings of others; 2) how your disease affected your family; 3) how your disease affected your social life; 4) how your disease affected your finances; 5) how your disease affected your job or career; 6) dangerous situations and accidents while under the influence; 7) moments you felt terror and fear; 8) the financial cost of your disease." This was a lot of work. Nearly each one of us had been a very successful student, but this assignment was very difficult because we had to talk about feelings and how we affected others. It was hard to get. The understanding required was usually beyond us until we had delivered.

What was not hard to get was the tension in that room every day at 9:15 a.m. Usually Karen, the monster-dancer-recovery Nazi, ran the delivery. All of the patients would be assembled, whispering about the deliverer of the day. "He's still using...." "Karen is out for her...." "Karen's in a bad mood...." "I'm glad it's not me today." Then Karen herself would quietly come in. She would sit in a chair very close to the exit door. She would say nothing, but the whispers would stop right away. No one moved during the first step. Sometimes she would smile, but most often she would not. About once every two months she would announce in the voice of an artillery field commander which had to be heard over exploding shells, and which commanded immediate obedience: "For those of you new, here are the rules: You do not fidget; you do not move; you do not whisper; you do not talk; you do not chew gum; you do not leave; you do not come in late; you do not read; you do not write. All you do is listen. Nothing: books, purses, jackets...nothing is allowed on your laps. You do not make a comment until after the person delivering the first step has handed over his or her last piece of paper. Then you do not criticize. Instead, you only tell the group how you are reminded of what you do while using, and then you are to give a specific example of what your memory was. Then you will thank the deliverer for being honest enough to have made an impression on your foggy memories and confused sense of morality, so that you too may get in touch with your disease and its consequences. Do not story tell. I am not interested in the dramatic bullshit of your life." Then she would close those rules by saying, "I will not abide whining, and I will stop the first step delivery if I hear any whining." Usually, all she would say is: "Begin." The fear wasn't so much in delivering the first step as it was in hearing Karen's analysis and comments after all else was said.

When I first heard a "First Step", I was just out of the hospital and still feeling the effects of the detox drugs. I hardly knew anyone yet, and sat in one of the chairs pushed close up against the wall. I didn't know what to expect. I don't remember much of the presentation, but I remember one of the other patients commenting, saying: "That reminds me of the time my mother was in the hospital, unconscious, dying of cancer. I put a needle into her IV bag and withdrew the morphine and replaced it with salt water." I was shocked. There is no other word for my reaction. I physically felt as though I had been hit.

I later spoke with Eddy about it, wanting him to approve my judgment that the commentator was a horrible person. He looked at me and said: "You're going to hear a lot of stuff like that. Especially from the medical people, the doctors, nurses and pharmacists." I was still shocked and said so. He said: "Ron, who's to say what you or I would have done if we had the knowledge or opportunity. We're drunks, but we can get alcohol. Imagine working in a liquor store where you could choose anything you wanted to drink and no one could tell if you were drunk! Wouldn't you do it? I can't say I wouldn't have done the same thing." I started to calm down, realizing he was probably right. Then he laughed and said, "And, after all, she was dying! It's not like it would have kept her alive." I must have looked beyond shock. Then he said: "Just kidding, man," while he walked out of the room. I wasn't so sure.

Later that week a young looking woman gave her first step. She identified herself as a housewife, but she was very, very rich and had homes all over the world. She was on her third marriage. Her first two husbands had died from combinations of drugs, booze and reckless behavior. I think she was rich before she met either of them, but I'm not sure. Her manners were exquisite, so I think she was raised in the nether world of responsibility where she was taken care of by others. From the way she talked, it seemed that she had not lost her ability to connect with her children and those who loved her. She had an air of tragedy, sorrow and dignified grace.

I still felt isolated and alone as I heard her story even though I was surrounded by at least fifty other patients, some of whom I knew by name. She wore a very subdued, muted silk suit that looked as though she wore it normally to board meetings of charities and hospitals. She smiled, ran her hand behind her skirt as she sat down, and then sat with her legs crossed at the ankle and tucked underneath the chair. She looked down at the yellow sheets of paper in her lap, looked up at us again and smiled as though she were going to deliver the minutes from the last board meeting or give a report on how much money the Pink Ball had raised. Instead, she said: "My name is Julia and this is my first step." She pronounced every syllable in her first name and made it sound like a song.

"Dangerous situations: My children, my fiancé, my sister and I were on our boat in Belize. The children and I were certified divers, but we hired a dive-master to show us the coral. I had nothing to eat for breakfast but champagne and orange juice. I lied to the dive-master and told him I had not been drinking. I also took a handful of pills. When we were in the water, we were not supposed to go deeper than fifteen feet because my sister and fiancé were new to diving. I tried to show off and dove to the bottom which was about sixty-five feet. I passed out while in the water. I have no memory of getting to the surface but was told later that my son and the dive-master came down together to get me. As they got me on board, I vomited so much only bile would come out. For the rest of the trip no one would even go near the water."

"Family: My children were home from school. We had planned to meet my parents and drive with them to our home in the country and spend a week together. We had not been together for months. My son was putting the luggage in the trunk and on the luggage rack. As I got in the car, I stumbled. My daughter looked at me and said: 'Are you okay?' I said, 'Yes, honey, I just have a little headache.' She looked at me to see if I were lying. As we got into the car, I reached into my pocket and took a pill. I wasn't sure what it was. My son saw me and said: 'We're not going anywhere with you. You're taking pills.' I told him he was mistaken. He started shouting at me. I slapped him across the face and shoved him in the car. I pushed my daughter in and drove off leaving the luggage in the drive with the other bags sliding off the roof. My daughter was crying. My son was grabbing for the wheel. By the end of the block, I ran into a ditch, then drove over a neighbor's yard, hitting their car. None of us were physically hurt. My parents came to get the children. My parents and my children told me they would never drive with me again."

"Family: My daughter gave a recital at her school which my fiancé and I flew to attend. I had taken a handful of pills as we landed, because I had a headache. Again, I did not know what they were. During the middle of her recitation, I felt dizzy and stood to get some air. I fell backwards and fell onto the people behind me. I could not stand up and kept saying: 'shhss!' thinking no one else had noticed. The people behind me helped me stand up. I then noticed that my daughter had quit playing. I tried to smile at her but vomited, staining my clothes and spraying the people around me with my vomit. My daughter ran crying off the stage. She has quit taking music lessons and playing her instrument. She will not even listen to music. If there is music on when we are together, she will turn it off or leave the room." She told these stories so calmly and with apparent disinterest, yet she had tears streaming down her face. As she spoke more, she cried more. Her nose ran and she used the sleeve of her suit to wipe it. She used the cuff to wipe her tears so she could continue to read.

"Family and Social: We were all in Italy and were going to dine with a Cardinal, who was a friend of my fiancé. I had been drinking secretly all day while also taking more pills."

She stopped talking for a moment and briefly closed her eyes.

She took a deep breath and continued: "My family are very devout Catholics and the children were looking forward to the dinner. We got to the Cardinal's palace and were shown into his sitting room."

No one in the all-purpose room was moving. The drinking and pill taking were common to us but not the backdrop, not the scenery, not the incredible and, what appeared to be, emotional honesty. She looked down at her yellow sheets which she was now clutching with both hands. "The Cardinal came in and offered us cocktails. Everyone looked at me and I said: 'It would be impolite to refuse.' He offered sherry, but I asked for vodka, which he had. I drank it and commented on the beauty of his palace and the magnificence of the art. My children and my fiancé became quiet. I reached into my pocket and took out more pills which I swallowed. The Cardinal spoke about the majesty of God and how He was reflected in the artwork. I looked at him and said: 'Fuck God! God took away my husbands; God took away my children's father. God left me nothing but misery.' I took a small statue and threw it on the floor. I took my glass and threw it at a painting. I kept screaming 'Fuck God. Fuck God.'"

She kept saying "fuck God" over and over again. The rest of us were crying now. Some, including myself, were sobbing. She continued: "My children and my fiancé tried to grab me. They tried to hug me. I kicked them and continued shouting. The Cardinal came over and hugged me too, saying: 'God loves you.' I sobbed, 'if God loved me, I would not be like this.' My children kept saying: 'We love you. Momma, we love you.' The Cardinal said: 'Because God loves you, He has made you like this. I was on my hands and knees with them hugging me and crying themselves. I screamed 'Fuck God.'"

"Fuck God. Fuck God." she said as she sobbed and as her head lowered. She stopped speaking. She slowly raised her head and passed her yellow sheets to the person next to her. No one else moved. There was no sound except for the crying and the sobbing. No one said anything. Those who could stared at the large red second hand which barely moved. Those who couldn't just stared. Then a very petite woman cleared her voice. She took an audible breath and said: "I thought God had given me nothing but a life of punishment too. I thought I was alone. Thank you for letting me know that I wasn't."

I was still crying so much that I could not clearly see. I looked at where Julia sat and said: "I used to pray as I fell asleep every night: 'God, let me die tonight.' I thought I was alone until just now. Thank you, Julia."

Then no one else said anything but sobs were still audible. I looked at Karen who sat unmoving, staring at Julia. A middle-aged, white haired and bearded man said: "Thank you, Julia. You have reminded me of the time I hit my son the night of his high school graduation party. Thank you for reminding me." There were a few other comments like that, but the silence returned.

Karen looked down at a watch in her hand and said: "That's very moving. You know, I noticed that the reactions of the other patients were more openly honest than yours. Their tears seemed more real to me somehow. I was really struck by how many were silent and didn't make comments. I wonder how many identified more with your kids than with you. You are so out of touch with reality, painting yourself as a victim of God. Of course you drink, devastate your children and are addicted to pills. God has cursed you."

I was shocked by the intensity of Karen's comments and by her perception. I had identified more with the children. That's who my tears were for. I had not realized my own feelings until she spoke.

"You say you don't know what pills you take, that you just have handfuls in your pocket? How many treatment centers have you been in? You know more about pills than pharmacists. You say God has cursed you. He gave you brains, beauty, money and the ability to act. How many first steps have you delivered? Your script is so polished that it would be a fantastic movie of the week. But you know what, Julia? There's not an actress good enough to play you except you or maybe another addict like Judy Garland, but she's dead. Think of the sets: the boat on Belize; the racing Mercedes or whatever else rich person car you drive; the Cardinal's palace. How romantic: Only being able to have champagne and orange juice for breakfast. How disadvantaged. What a curse."

"I've heard bullshit before, but it's been a long time since I've heard such a florid tapestry of bullshit. You aren't in touch with your feelings or the disastrous consequences to your children and family. You think the only thing that happened to your daughter was losing her interest in music? That's the least thing that's happened to her. While you were being Judy Garland and throwing up in public, your kids were learning how to be Kurt Cobain and Liza Minnelli. What great futures they're going to have."

"Do you have to do your First Step again? I don't know. Maybe. I don't know if you can get in any more touch with your feelings right now than you have. Your disease is so strong and you love being the victim. What a victim. You're not a victim, you're a victimizer.

Why don't you ask some of the real victims here if they'll change places with you. Why don't you go ask the crack addicts down by the airport if they'll change places with you. You think God had cursed you by giving you what anyone else would take as a blessing. You are as shallow and selfish as anyone I've seen. We have a saying in recovery: You don't get well if you're too smart, too young or too rich. There may be some hope for you. You're still here, and you haven't walked out yet. That's a smile sign of progress."

"Instead of being angry at God, why don't you make a gratitude list? You need to get on your knees and show some gratitude."

At that Karen stood up, looked one last time at Julia, and then said to her: "Lead us in the Serenity Prayer. And no bullshit from any of you."

Andy and the Snake

Andy was so fascinated by animals. Every day he told us about snakes, dogs, cats and those other animals someone raised in cities he knows. He spoke with the passion of an animal rights activist, the knowledge of a biologist and, frankly, with the twisted love of a stalker.

He read me a story from his journal. He said it was a true story of his own past. He had been living in a new neighborhood in what recently been country and near wilderness in Texas. He was about 14 and had no friends, except his little brother who was less of a friend and more of a punching bag tension reliever for Andy. From living with Andy and hearing his stories, I'm sure his brother ran when he knew Andy was nearby. On this particular day, Andy was bored. It was a little before he became a drug addict, and his brother wasn't around to receive Andy's attentions and divert his boredom. Andy went for a walk out past the new neighborhood and into what natural land was left.

This was an area where the dirt on the ground was thin. You could kick the dirt off with the toe of your boot. Underneath, you'd find rock. The dirt couldn't support much growth but the weeds didn't care. They grew tall and deep. There was a stream which ran from the undeveloped into the developed. As it approached the neighborhood, the stream was diverted into a large pipe where it disappeared under the ground. The banks of the stream were deep, which was fortunate, because when it rained the stream became a forceful and dangerous river. Andy and all the kids in the neighborhood were told every day to stay away from it. Since he was bored, Andy went right to it.

On his way, he saw a huge snake. He told me it must have been at least six feet long. It slithered along the bank of the stream, in and out of the weeds. It glowed and shined when the sun struck it. Its scales were like armor which held all colors and released them at the speed of light, but one at a time. Andy's eyes could not leave it. He thought the snake was a special present from God to him. He followed it until it went down the bank of the stream. The bank was shale, crumbly and dangerous. It was dotted with potholes and caves. Clumps of weeds grew from the sides. Andy stood there and watched the snake. It had stopped. Even still, though, it still glittered, glowed and shined.

Andy was in a trance that he wouldn't reach again until he started shooting cocaine into his bloodstream while mixing it just right with LSD. He didn't hear the cars come up behind him. He didn't move until a rock hit him from behind.

"Hey!" he said. "What the fuck are you doing?" He turned and saw a group of young guys with some girls. There were about five guys and three girls, none of whom looked to be over twenty. He thought he recognized some of them from school.

"Who's saying fuck?" said one guy, who was also looking bored. Andy could smell the need for blood excitement on that guy too, but he was cautious. "Hey, I did" said Andy. Then he immediately said: "There's a snake over there so big I bet you'd never touch it." Everyone immediately looked to where the snake was. The guy said: "What the fuck you talkin' about? I don't need to touch it to kill it." Then he went to a car and brought out a little pistol. He took aim and shot at the snake. He missed, but shale splinters went everywhere. It looked as though the snake went just as fast down the sides of the bank and into a cave.

The guy said: "What snake?" and then turned to look at Andy, with the pistol still in his hand. "You got another snake I can shoot?" he said to Andy. Andy said: "No. But I can get you that snake." All the guys started to laugh and call him names. No one could get down the bank except a snake. Andy said: "If I get down there and get the snake you gotta give me your gun." The guy said: "No way, man." Andy said: "You scared I can do it?" In front of his group, the guy said: "okay. Go for it. You get that snake and bring it up here and you can have my gun." Andy said: "okay."

Andy told me he had no fear. Or if he had it, he never listened to it about stuff like this. He walked to the edge of the bank. He walked and slid down to the cave where he saw the snake went in. The angle was so steep, the guys and girls on the bank could hardly see him. They kept yelling at him. "Stupid" "Dumb fuck" "Chicken." Andy said nothing. Knowing him now, I'm sure he had this intense, death grip grin on his face.

He slowed down as he got to the cave. He went around it carefully. Then he leaned into the bank and slowly crawled up to it. The cave was huge. If the sun had not been rising, no one would have seen the cave. If the sun had not been rising, no one could have seen inside it. But Andy saw inside it. He saw the snake just inside the entrance. He saw it shimmering and glittering in the sun against the black background of the unseen cave walls. He saw it relax, coil its six feet of length against itself like a dog does when it wants to preserve its own body heat. He saw the snake move its mouth as though it were yawning. He saw its green eyes stare at nothing. He saw it, and then he grabbed it and then he killed it by smashing its head on the rock floor of the cave.

He had stopped hearing the cries of the kids up on the road, but now he heard them again. One insistent cry of "Hey man!" kept coming through. He yelled back: "I'm on my way up." New questions were yelled at him: "Did you get it?" which were answered by others: "No way, man. No way could he get that snake." The gun guy said: "He's chicken and stupid anyway." Andy said nothing as he crawled and slide up the bank. He needed both hands so he wrapped the dead snake around his neck as he crawled up the shale on hands and knees, cutting the palms of his hands and the tops of his knees. He started sweating and wiped the sweat from his forehead with one bloody hand and then the other. He got to the overhang of the bank and stopped. No one could see him. He got his breath and then laid one leg over the overhang and pushed himself up with the other.

The guys and girls were startled. No one said anything, but Andy grinned. The gun guy still had his gun in his hand but he dropped his jaw. The girls all looked at him like he was more than just an attractive nuisance. The gun guy said: "Well, that's cool man, but you ain't getting my gun." Andy said: "You promised." "Promises to nuts don't count." Andy walked to the guy and said: "Don't make promises you can't keep." The guy backed up a step or two and started to raise his gun: "Get away from me, man." Andy said nothing but kept walking. As he did, he unwrapped the dead snake, now colored only grey but still huge, and threw it at the gun guy. He threw up his hands to keep the snake away and fell backwards with the snake on him. Andy leaned over, picked up the gun and said: "You can keep the snake, man. It's no good now anyway." The other guys and girls laughed. The gun guy stood up and said: "Hey give me my gun back." Andy said: "My gun. You got a snake. Shoot it." The gun guy looked as though he were going to start a fight, but Andy got that look again which made his own brother run from him. Another guy, a big guy, said: "Cool it. You promised him your gun for the snake and he delivered." He then looked at Andy and said: "See you around, man." Everyone got in their cars and left. One girl looked back through the rear window of the car she was in. She smiled and waved. Andy walked home with the gun in his hand and with the grin on his face.

Games

The most exercise addicts got was running to get their drug and running away from the consequences of using it. The treatment center did not approve of that kind of exercise so regular "fun" exercise was required. This meant at least weekly softball games, bowling, roller skating or golf, of which each one I hated. Watching them, though, was great. I don't know which sport had more uncoordinated, grandiose former experts telling everyone else what to do. The "if onlys" of blame placed by one patient in treatment upon another were probably only surpassed by Napoleon blaming his marshals, Hitler blaming his generals or Nixon blaming the press.

There was a thrill in watching a former professional athlete miss the hit, drop the bowling ball, skid the skate or swing the club with the force of a Scotsman throwing a log, only to hit empty air. Screwball comedies and Stooges remakes could easily be cast with patients in treatment. What I did instead of playing was to watch and comment with sideways glee. I was joined in this by a married woman named Pam, who was evil in that she did nothing but encourage me. Normally men and women were segregated in all activities except for treatment and organized exercises. We couldn't even eat lunch together, but when it came to exercise we could speak, touch and laugh.

Pam did play one physical game, but that was before she discovered life in the bleachers with Ron. I saw that game and she was great. I was still detoxing, and I'm pretty sure she was too. Tony, in a perpetual state of detox, denial or use, had told everyone how great he was and how he had this secret prayer to make sure he got a hit. I think Tony used to crawl the pages of obscure religious texts to find specific prayers to justify his desires and grant his wishes. From what I hear, he's now trying to put all those prayers on a CD so that all other addicts and alcoholics can just type in a word on a computer and some super-wunderkind search engine will scan not only his archives but those of the Vatican and as-yet undiscovered caves in Jerusalem. That day Tony said a prayer to let him hit a big one but to have somebody else do the actual physical work of running because both of his knees were gone. Pam walked by as he was quite publicly and loudly saying his prayer.

"Tony," she called, "what is this shit you're mumbling?"

"Pam, it's not shit. It's a Veda in which I ask Krishna to send me Arjuna to run the bases for me."

Pam started to giggle so hard she was squeezing her eyes. She said: "I know Krishna, but this Arjuna must be one of those guys I haven't met yet." Tony gave her such a look of condescension I thought she would melt like ice cream in the Georgia sun, but either the look didn't connect or she just didn't care. Pam said: "Why do you need help?" Tony said: "Both of my knees were wrecked in surgery by some incompetent, and I can't run without bone crunching on bone."

I was sitting right next to them and couldn't keep still. "Tony, I heard your knees got wrecked by giving too many blow jobs while kneeling on concrete to get crack or bending over to let your dealers get at yours. It's horrible not having money, isn't it?" Tony looked at me with more than murderous intent and stood up with true rage. I said: "Tony, if you want to do me harm, you're gonna have to chase me. But then maybe that's Krishna's way of hearing your prayers." Tony said:

"Fucking fag."

I said, "Ah, Tony, that's a wish and an activity not limited to fags."

Pam was waving her right arm like it was signaling the beginning of a fit so we all paid attention to her to see if maybe she would do a devil's dance on the diamond, but she took great heaps of breath, wiped her eyes and said: "Tony, I'll be glad to run for you, and then I'm going to sit down with Ron."

Tony grabbed the bat, which he held with a severe choke. I yelled: "Where did you learn to hold a bat like that? Practicing on your wife's neck?" He didn't answer but swung at the first ball. He got a hit. It only went about three inches and was judged a foul ball anyway. Pam was still laughing but took up her position and yelled: "C'mon Tony! C'mon Krishna! C'mon Arjuna!" Tony swung again but this time Krishna himself must have grabbed the bat because it was vertical while the ball was on the horizontal.

I said: "Tony, I think you forgot the incense and to paint yourself blue. Krishna is sending you a signal." Tony didn't look at me, but stood still twisting his hands on the bat. Pam started laughing. She said: "Why blue?" "Well, Pam," I said, "Krishna is always painted blue. Probably because he's separated from his lovers like Tony."

Tony walked up to the plate again, got into the best batter position his defective knees would allow, and not only swung at the ball, he got a hit! The addicts in the outfield were talking about something amongst themselves (most certainly various drugs and great highs) so no one caught it. Pam ran from home plate just like a giggling girl, which made sense because that's exactly what she was at that moment. The outfielders were looking for the ball and the catcher kept screaming at them. It was Brand. I should have known. He was pointing to where the ball sat, underneath a new patient's pant cuffs. I mean underneath, too. The new patient was a young woman who wore platform shoes and bell bottoms so wide they would have hidden a baby elephant. She had short black hair with spit curls held in place by bobby pins and a red ribbon bow pinned in place over her left ear. Brand was screaming at her: "Pick up the ball! Pick up the ball!!! She slowly leaned over and said: "Yeah, yeah. Just relax a little, will 'ya? If I bend over too fast there ain't no guarantee I can get up again."

Brand was really going nuts and so was Tony. They were both screaming at the woman helping them, or screwing them up, depending upon perspective. Tony said: "Go, Pam, go! Stop laughing and run!" She was laughing so hard I thought she'd roll over, but she kept running. Brand was turning red and then blue, whether from lack of oxygen or Tony's request for a visitation from Krishna I don't know. The new patient leaned over and gingerly picked up the ball. Her fingernails were painted black and were so long they curved.

"Pick it up! Pick it up!" demanded Brand.

"I don't know who you are kid," she said, "but these nails took a year to grow so tone it down and lighten it up a little! Jesus! If you were sucking your energy from Con-Ed, New York would be having a black out right now!"

She couldn't get hold of the ball with one hand, so she used the palms of both hands to pick it up. Then she held it over her head and yelled: "Hey! Look'it me! I'm a ball player!" She turned around in a circle, holding the ball over her head, held gingerly yet securely between her palms, as though she were holding up an Academy Award or a magic orb. All the players and everyone in the bleachers stood and cheered.

Pam had just passed third bass and was on her way home. Instead of running, she started skipping. Tony yelled at her: "Run! Run! Run!"

Brand really was turning blue: "Throw the fucking ball, you bitch!" The new patient looked at Brand with a "fuck you" look which she immediately supported by saying: "Hey, cretin, I don't know who you are, but you need to relax."

Brand yelled: "Fuck you bitch, give me the ball!"

She said: "Fuck me? You think you could fuck me? Not when I got your ball in my hand." She started laughing, too. Then she said: "Hey, look at her skip, will 'ya? Doing her Dorothy imitation. If we only had a fucking dog. Jesus, that looks like fun." Still holding the ball over her head, she started skipping toward Brand.

While she was doing that, Pam crossed home plate and Tony hugged her. Everyone applauded. The new patient kept skipping towards home plate, and Brand, who stood there, was vibrating in place. Pam put her hand on his shoulder and said: "Hey, Brand, it's okay. It's just a game."

"Yeah, it's easy to see that's what you think it is." He tore her hand off his shoulder. Pam just looked at him and walked back toward me. I put my arms around her and lifted her off the ground. We both looked at the new patient. I asked Pam: "What's her name."

Pam giggled and said: "You won't believe this, but it's Glenda." I sang: "She's off to see the bastard, the wonderful bastard of Brand." Pam joined in and so did a few others.

When Glenda got to home plate, she stopped skipping and walked the few remaining steps to where Brand stood. She was a midget compared to him. The ball was still over her head. Her bracelets were stacked at her elbows. She just stood there. He glared at her. No one said anything. The glee was gone from the moment. One of the counselors started walking slowly to where they stood.

Glenda said: "You call me bitch? Did I hear you right?" He said: "I called you what I called you." She said: "You call me a bitch! Listen, you still want your ball?"

He said: "Yeah." She didn't move a muscle nor drop her stare. She said: "Beg for it, bitch."

This, I thought, was getting dangerous. Then Pam started to giggle and so did the rest of the women. The counselor, who was also a woman, stopped moving. She didn't giggle, but she did smile.

Brand said nothing, but I think he was turning blue again. She said: "You know, my granddad fought in a war for guys like you. If he met you, I think he'd be sorry he won." We all laughed at that one. She still held the ball head high but moved it forward a few inches. "You want your ball," she said, "go get it." Then she dropped it at her feet. "I don't want it no more anyway. I think it's got mold and green stuff all over it." She walked closer to Brand and said: "Boo!" Then she walked away.

The counselor came over and said: "okay. It's time we changed teams anyway and took a break." Glenda giggled and skipped to the bleachers, where she sat down. Brand stood there like a statue. The counselor went up to him and said something very quietly. He didn't move. She audibly said: "Now." He walked away so stiffly I thought his bones would break. He sat in the top of the bleachers.

Pam and I were giggling again and the counselor came over to us. "Okay, you two. I'm putting you on restrictions until tomorrow. No contact between the two of you until you each talk with your primary."

I was shocked. "Jeez! I thought you guys wanted me to learn to like women."

The counselor, whose name I did not know, said: "That's enough or I'll put you on sarcasm restriction." Pam said: "Ron, it's okay. You'll die if that happens. The game is about over anyway."

The next morning, in primary group, Cliff went through the checklist on his clipboard, telling the other patients stuff like: "You need to spend more time on the third step. Go see Father Liam." He made all the rounds and saved me for last. He put his clipboard down, leaned back and started playing with his shoes, pushing the heel of one down with the toe of the other. I knew something was coming. "What's this I hear about you nearly inciting a riot yesterday?"

I was totally bewildered. "What are you talking about?"

He said: "You're not a good liar, so don't even try."

"Cliff," I said, "I'm not lying. I don't know what you're talking about." He looked at his watch. "We don't have time to get into it now. Meet me in my office in an hour."

So for the next hour all I did was worry. I found Pam in the lounge eating potato chips and drinking coffee. I'd never seen anyone eat chips and drink coffee. I said: "Pam, can I talk with you?" She said: "Sure, love, what's up?"

The "love" word bothered me, because I sure didn't love her as much as I liked her. I knew it was just a figure of speech left over from the Liverpool influence of John, George, Paul and Ringo, but it still bothered me.

I said: "Cliff wants me in his office. He says I was 'inciting a riot' yesterday. All I remember doing is laughing with you."

She said: "Yeah, I already got blasted by my primary. They think that we undermined the entire purpose of the game, which is to teach people how to get along. You and I were setting up a hierarchy of "cool kids" versus "un-cool kids.""

I looked at her and said: "Brand bitched." She said: "Yep." I said: "But Pam, he is an un-cool kid."

Andy had been laying on his stomach on one of the couches, apparently asleep, while I was talking with Pam. He rolled over on his back, threw an arm over his eyes and said: "Yeah, he's un-cool all right."

I said: "Andy, how can we tell when you're asleep or awake and eavesdropping?"

He kept his eyes covered but smiled. "You can't. But it's not like you've got a lot of secrets from me anyway." He continued: "By your laughter and jokes, you're diverting the other patients from building their own relationships. You're also keeping yourself from building 'normal' relationships. Sometimes you're just too damn funny for their own good. They're going to want to split you and Pam up, so you'll both probably go on joke restriction or something juvenile like that."

I said: "I just don't see what's so wrong about laughter." Andy started giggling. He still kept his eyes covered with his forearm and cleared his throat. "Oh, Ron, you are so sick! If you laugh, they tell you not to. If you don't laugh, they tell you to find the humor. I'll bet you

Brand ran right to Cliff or the counselor on call and said you made fun of him and that you being here is interfering with his recovery. I'll bet they told him to learn to laugh. They're just trying to get us to rid ourselves of our default behaviors."

Pam jammed some chips in her mouth and said, "Yeah, Andy, like you pretending to be asleep a lot."

Andy giggled again and said: "Well, I wake up whenever I hear bullshit and that's just about any time Ron talks. It's multiplied when the two of you are together."

I looked at him. He hadn't changed his clothes for at least three days. He had on drab olive green pants which were stained with dark patches of something. He had on expensive but filthy work boots, a long-sleeved white T-shirt over which he had a bright yellow short-sleeved T-shirt. His hair was about the same color as the yellow shirt and was a matted mess.

"Andy, when was the last time you took a shower?"

"Ron," he said, "you're just asking me a personal hygiene question to divert attention from your own failings. And I know it's your fantasy to see me naked in the shower, but that's not going to happen."

He was right, but I said: "Andy, your fantasy is wishing that were my fantasy. I like my guys clean."

Pam said: "Andy, do you always flirt and manipulate when you pretend to be asleep?" He laughed and rolled over on his stomach.

Pam jammed some more chips in her mouth and said: "Don't worry about it. It's not like Cliff is going to shoot you."

"No," I said, "it's worse than that. He might tell me something truthful about myself."

I went outside and stood in the sun. It was so hot. Back home the air would smell clean and crisp because it was autumn. Here it was a perpetual summer. There was the smell of the pines, but it was intermixed with a decaying smell of overripe vegetation gone on too long. I got too hot so I went inside where I sat on the hallway floor across from Cliff's office.

He came walking along about fifteen minutes later. He looked down at me and said: "Aren't you afraid of being run over sitting down there like that?" I said: "Should I be? Are you going to run me over?"

He pulled his head back a little and said: "Is that what you think?" I stood up, smiling, and said: "I don't know what to think." He opened the door to his office and motioned me in.

His office had a window but the blinds were drawn and only a little natural light came in. He had an enormous real wood desk with a computer and pictures of himself with a woman and a little boy. There was a smaller desk perpendicular to his which also had a computer, but nothing else. There was a straight-backed chair right next to Cliff's, and he motioned me to it. He sat in the swivel chair at his desk.

I said: "Why don't you open your blinds?" He said: "If I did, every addict in the place would spend all day walking back and forth to see who was in here with me. Then they'd pump the person who was in here to see what I had said. Then they'd start rumors."

I said: "Are you serious?"

"You tell me."

I laughed and said: "Well, I wouldn't keep walking by but, sure, I'd look in when I did walk by, and I'd listen to the gossip."

He said: "I bet. I'll also bet you've figured out why I wanted to talk to you too, right?"

"I don't know why you want to talk with me," I said, putting a strong emphasis on the word "know," "but from what I hear you think that I've been making fun of other patients at their expense."

He said: "Well, is that true?" "Not true," I responded. "I haven't been making fun of anyone." "C'mon, Ron," he said, "One of the counselors saw what you and Pam did yesterday."

"Cliff," I said, "all I did was laugh at other people who were being funny." "Yeah," he said. "And all you did was set them up to be funny, and all you did was encourage others to think they were funny, and all you did was not care how sick the funny guy was."

"You mean Tony?" I asked. "Actually," he said, "you choose, because I should have said men and women." I said: "Well, no matter what I did, I don't see how I was inciting a riot."

He pushed his chair a little away from his desk and turned in it to sit exactly across from me. He leaned back, stretched out his legs and started playing with his shoes again, pulling the heel of one off with the toe of the other. He said: "Okay, I'll agree it wasn't a riot. But you weren't playing the game either. You were distracting the people who were playing."

"Cliff," I said, "isn't this really about how Glenda got Brand so pissed?"

He smiled and said: "He is easy to piss off."

"So," I asked, "am I supposed to walk around on egg shells worrying what his reaction to me might be? I've walked on eggshells my whole life."

"No," he said, "we don't want you to walk on egg shells, but we don't want you to walk into a fist either." "So," I asked, "are you telling me I am physically unsafe because of Brand?" "No," he said again. "Brand knows the second he touches someone the police are called and he's out of here."

I felt queasy, "You mean, he's already under some kind of court order regarding violence?"

"Ron, what I mean is that you are physically safe. If any patient, or staff member for that matter, ever touched you or threatened to do so, that person would be dismissed immediately."

He paused. Then he asked, "Do you mind if I tell you a personal story?"

I started to automatically say, "Sure," but I caught myself. I sat there for a moment and said: "You know, when I first got here, I would have said: 'go right ahead,' but then I would have used whatever personal information you gave me to analyze and manipulate you."

He said "you think you can manipulate me?"

I said: "Of course. Now don't get up on your excited macho horse. Any of us can. If you don't realize or can't admit that, then you're already being manipulated."

He sat still and said: "Go on."

"So, Cliff, I'd just as soon not know anything about your life, then I can take your advice and comments for just what they appear to be. I don't even like knowing that you have a wife and one child you adore."

He said: "What makes you say that?"

I laughed, "Cliff, you've got photos of you, a woman your age, and a child who could be your clone, all over your desk. You've got two toys for kids on it. You have the goofy 'does it get any better than this look' on your face in the photos. See what I do with just a little information? If I know too much about you, I will automatically use that information to discount the stuff I don't want to hear. I'll think more about you and tangential meanings than just accepting what you have to say. If you don't mind, I'd just as soon keep our relationship pure for a while anyway. How about I let you know when I think I'm solid enough to hear about your life?"

Cliff sat still for a while and said: "okay. But you have to promise me that if you do find your mind working overtime about what I've said, you will find me, and sit with me, and tell me what you're thinking."

I said: "okay. Is that it?"

He said: "It? We've hardly just begun. I'm placing you on organized sports restrictions. No more group games for you."

I laughed and said: "Well, if that's supposed to hurt, it doesn't."

He said: "No, I didn't think it would nor did I want it to. But, you have to play golf with Father Liam at least once a week."

"Cliff," I said, "this is running towards punishment. I really don't like golf, I'm not much of a golfer and I'm not sure I trust him."

Cliff said: "You've been golfing with Andy a couple of times here and just because one priest may have abused you doesn't mean they all will."

I sat still. "Cliff," I said, "I never told anyone that. I didn't even put it on your form."

He said: "Yeah, I know. But no one has such a continuous negative reaction as you do without some kind of reason. This is not just my decision. This is a staff decision."

I asked, "What does that mean?"

"It means," he answered, "that all of the counselors have discussed this and agree."

"All this for making fun of Tony and Brand?" I asked.

He said, "Nope. This was being discussed the first day you got here. You just showed us the way, that's all."

I said, "So, what do I do?" He answered, "You see Liam before the end of the day and make arrangements."

I must have looked upset because he said: "How are you feeling?" When I said nothing he said: "Mad, sad, glad or afraid? Or all of the above?"

I said" "I'm not really mad. I'm not sad, and I'm certainly not glad. I'm a little afraid. I just keeping thinking how uncomfortable I feel with priests."

He gently kicked the side of my shoe with the toe of his. "Don't worry," he said. "He'll ask Andy and Kevin to go along, you won't be left alone with a priest. Does that make you feel better?"

"Yes," I said, "it makes me feel a lot better."

Cliff smiled, stood up and said: "Okay, get out of here and find Liam before you find out more about me."

I smiled, stood up and said: "Okay, Obi-Wan, I'm on my way." I stopped at the door, turned around and said: "Is this a quest-journey-search for the Holy Grail kind of thing?"

He said: "It all is." I said: "okay" and left.

I walked down the hallway slowly. I looked into the lounge and saw that Andy was still on the couch, looking like he was asleep. I was tempted to go in and talk with him, but I thought that if I did, I would be rejecting Cliff's advice and concerns. So I walked around the building looking for Liam. I didn't see him so I asked the receptionist if she knew where he was.

She said: "Sure, honey," in a very languid, intimate way, "He's down in his office."

"Do you think I can just go down there?"

"Sure, honey, that's what he's there for."

His office was in the hospital building, right down from where the new patients checked in. Cliff's office door was solid wood, but Liam's was nearly all glass. He was sitting there at his desk reading what looked like a patient chart.

I knocked. He looked up, smiled and said: "Come on in!" I stuck my head in the doorway and he said: "Come on in means bring your whole body in. So bring all of you in and sit down."

I did that and said: "I'm Ron," to which he laughed and said: "Oh, I know who you are!" He emphasized every word of the sentence as though each one could stand alone, as though each word were its own independent sentence. "What can I do for you?" he asked.

I was afraid to talk with him, to establish any intimacy, so I said: "Why is your door glass and Cliff's wood?" He laughed and said: "Ah, what a wonderful way to avoid why you are here! Cliff's is wood to insure privacy. Mine is glass in case any of you checking in for the first time start to go crazy. I can see what's going on and then call for assistance in case the intake worker is overwhelmed."

"Does that happen often?" I asked.

He laughed again, "Often enough to justify putting in a glass door! Now that you know the purpose of our doors, what's the purpose of your visit?"

"I guess," I said, "I'm supposed to arrange a golf game with you." He laughed again and said: "Now that's a good one. You 'guess!' You mean you've been told!" "Well, yeah," I said.

"Who told you?" he said. "I have the feeling you already know," I answered. "After all, aren't you part of staff?" He chortled: "Yes, indeed I am!"

I said: "I'm not much of a golfer. And besides, what makes you think I can do it at all?"

He laughed again, "Mr. Lawyer, think. Did you have to get permission for your brother to bring your car down?"

"Yes," I said, "Cliff had to approve it."

"And," he continued, "Weren't you surprised to see your golf clubs in it when your brother arrived?"

"Yes," I said again.

"In fact," he said, "didn't you tell your brother it was a waste of space and time to bring them?" "Yes," I said. "I'm beginning to feel as though you guys have arranged all of this." "Ah," he said, "we're making progress because your feelings are right!"

I didn't say anything. I was a little angry at my family for talking with the staff without letting me know what was going on. I didn't say anything, so Liam said: "Don't be angry at your family. They love you and don't know what to do. So they trust us and listen to us. You might do as well to do so."

"Okay," I said, "I'm not going to fight what you guys do, and unless I bug all your offices, I'm not going to know what you say until you tell me." "Ah," he said, "Now you're beginning to realize that you can't control everything. Good. Well, right now I just want you to think about controlling the direction of a golf ball."

"Okay," I said, "what happens next?" Liam smiled and said: "We'll be taking Kevin and Andy with us since you all live in the same dome. I'll pick you up Saturday right after Real People. So be ready."

"Saturday?" I said. "I normally do the grocery shopping on Saturday." Liam said: "It's time you learned not to be such a caretaker. Either the other men will shop or you can do it on Sunday. I'll be in front of your dome on Saturday. Now get out of here, because I've got thinking to do." He smiled and said: "See you Saturday."

So I smiled and left. As I walked down the corridor, I noticed that all the doors in the corridor were glass. All of the offices but two were vacant. In one of them a middle-aged guy was lying on a couch staring at the ceiling. His right arm was lying on the floor motionless. He was raising his left arm up and down as though he were pumping something. In the other occupied office was a middle-aged woman sitting at a desk looking at a younger woman. The younger woman had long, thick, dishwater blond matted hair which clung to the sides of her face. Tears were streaming down her face. The older woman had an impassive look on her face. As I passed, she looked at me for just a split second, during which time I felt as though she were scanning me to see if I was a threat to her or just another person walking along the corridor perhaps on a quest.

Games with Faith

During Real People on Saturday morning, all I could think about was how much I did not want to spend the day with a priest on a golf course. Kevin was in his doctors' group, but Andy sat next to me and whispered stupid things to me like "he's going to rape you on the 5th hole. That's when they always do it because it's the hole farthest from the clubhouse." I refused to look at him, because I knew I would laugh or hit him. He kept making comments, and I was trying to pay attention to the other patients. One guy was saying he was afraid he was going to relapse, because he had a substantial credit with his drug dealer, who delivered. The guy said he had checked out airport connections and memorized when his dealer could arrive. Andy stopped razzing me once he heard this guy's dilemma. This is when I discovered another of Andy's talents. Besides laughing and talking at the same time, he could also laugh and drool.

Kathy and Ed were running the group together. Ed was a middle-aged black man who used to be a big dealer and user himself. He looked at the guy and said:

"You're serious that you got a credit with your dealer?" The guy said: "Yeah. I know he'll bring it here because he brought dope to every other rehab I've been in."

Ed moved his head slowly back and forth and sounded like he was humming. He said: "Hmmm. That's a lot of temptation." The guy said "Yeah. It's all I can think about. I've made all sorts of plans on how to meet him at the airport or how he can disguise himself to bring me the drugs." Ed said: "You've got to think about what happens after he brings you the drugs. You've got to play the tape of the drug experience from the beginning to the end. You cannot leave out the static after the high. What happens if you or he get arrested? After all, we're not talking about pizza delivery here. We're talking about breaking the law."

"The last time I got high was when I sold some drugs to a cop. He bought his bag of heroin," which Ed pronounced as 'heron,' as though the drug were the bird, "but he wouldn't taste it. I said to him 'you a cop?' and he said 'no,' but I knew he was. So I jammed my gun into his mouth and pulled back the trigger. I told him 'you either taste the drug or you taste a bullet. It's your choice. He snorted some, but I shoved his face into it and made him snort enough so that he could barely walk. That's when I left. That was over 20 years ago, but I still remember that high and the fear that went with it. I've never killed a man, but I sure could have that day. You willing to take that risk?"

The guy put his head down sheepishly, as though he had been given a lecture by his junior high school principal. He put his knees together and folded his hands on his lap. He didn't look at anyone when he said "No." As soon as he said that, Andy jumped up and said: "You're lying! All you can think about is getting high. You don't even think about getting arrested, and you don't care who dies as long as you can get high. I bet you've got airline timetables in your pocket."

Ed ordered: "Sit down, Andy." Then he looked at the guy and said: "Stand up." The guy looked at Ed like he was nuts but stood up. Ed said: "Now empty your pockets on the floor. Just take whatever is in your pockets and drop them. And if you don't empty them, I will." The guy did just that. No airline schedules fell out: Keys, a wallet, some chapstick and some change. That was it. Ed looked at him and said: "Hmmm. I told you I'd come over there and do it for you. I'm gonna give you one more chance." I was surprised because it looked to me like he had reached into all his pockets. Ed said: "What's in your back pocket?" The guy said: "Nothing." Ed stood up, quickly walked across the room and reached into the guy's back pocket. He pulled out a folded, torn yellow piece of paper. "What's this?" he asked. The guy said nothing. Ed unfolded it. He looked at the guy who then hung his head. He started to sit down. Ed said: "Don't you be sitting down yet." Ed walked back to his chair. Andy was grinning and was becoming uncontained. As Ed walked by Andy, he handed him the piece of paper. Ed sat down and said: "Andy, why don't you tell us what that piece of paper is."

Andy laughed and said: "It's torn from the Yellow Pages. It's the page with all the numbers for all the airlines." Ed looked at Andy and said: "Give him back his piece of paper." Andy looked at Ed, smiled and walked across the room. He handed the torn page to the guy who just hung onto it. His face was red and he looked at Andy as though he expected Andy to explain it all to him. Andy went back to his chair and sat down. Ed then looked at the guy and said: "Since you're standing up already, why don't you just leave?" The guy's face went from red to white. He said something, but I couldn't hear it. Ed said: "What?" The guy said nothing. Ed said: "I told you. Go. Leave. Now. Ain't nobody going to stop you."

The guy didn't move. No one said anything. Andy started laughing again. Ed said: "Andy, why don't you tell us why he's just standing there like a dumb ass." Andy kept laughing and said: "He can't leave, because he's got nowhere to go and he's afraid. But his drug won't let him sit down either. He's frozen." Ed said: "Hmmm. Well, if you won't leave, then sit down, but we'll be putting you under surveillance. You understand?" The guy nodded his head. "That means no unmonitored phone calls, no unread letters, being with two other guys all the time. You'll be taking shits and showers with the bathroom door open. You got it?" The guy nodded yes again. "All right. Sit down."

Andy stopped whispering things to me, but he had a glazed look on his face. Ed looked over at me and said: "You playing golf with Andy and Liam today?" I said: "Yes. As soon as we get out of here." Ed said: "Tell Liam what happened here and don't let Andy be alone until you do." Andy laughed again and said: "God, Ed, you're right. If I'm left alone I'll get that dealer to come down here and make deliveries to all of us!" Everyone started laughing. Ed waited for the laughter to die down and then he said: "okay. Let's stand for the Serenity Prayer." We all stood, draped our arms across each other, and said the prayer.

Andy and I walked out together and he said: "Boy, Ed is a genius! Only another serious addict would know what that guy had in his pocket." I said: "It all seemed like mind reading to me." Andy said: "That's because you're fucked up in a different way, but boy are you fucked up!"

When we got back to the apartment, Father Liam and Kevin were already there. They had loaded the clubs and Liam said: "How was Real People?" I told him what had happened and he just started laughing. He said: "Oh, Andy, I'm thinking you'd best sit in the front seat with me so I can see how Satan is planning to take you back." I was a little miffed that Andy got to sit in front. I thought that this day had been created for me and Liam. Then I thought that maybe he was taking care of the three of us at once. I sat directly behind him and Kevin sat next to me.

I said: "Liam, I'm not much of a golfer so I don't know about this. How about I just get a paper or a book and read while you guys play?" Liam laughed and said: "Oh, no, Ron." He made my name sound like it had three "Rs" at the beginning and an "h" before the "n." "You'd like nothing better than to isolate in the sun on the porch of a clubhouse. It looks like you're not, because you're outside, but your disease lives in isolation so it's with other people you'll be all day."

Liam's car was a huge black Cadillac. He was so short and his seat was up so far that it felt like I was in a limousine. I said: "How does a priest get a car like this? I thought you guys took a vow of poverty?" "Now, Ron," he said, "stop worrying about where my car and I fit in the firmament and think about where you fit." I thought for a moment and said: "I have no idea where I fit." He said: "That's right. That's why you're here. It's the way God planned it." Kevin said: "You know, Liam, I'm not Catholic but my wife is. She believes all that stuff too." Liam said: "And that's why she'll forgive you your transgressions, Kevin, because she believes."

I said nothing the rest of the ride. It took us about an hour to get to the course. Kevin said: "Liam, do you always drive this fast?" Liam said: "Of course. In Ireland, we can hardly drive at all, so American roads are a great luxury and temptation. I usually leave late so I have to speed so I can arrive early." Kevin said: "That sounds like the disease talking to me." Liam laughed loudly and said: "Of course it is!"

The course, which was in the hills of Georgia, was nearly abandoned. It was cold, cloudy and misty. The grass was so wet it soaked through shoes. Within minutes, my toes were wet and cold. It felt normal to me. I said to Liam: "Is this what Ireland is like?"

"Oh," which he pronounced as "ooooo," "no. Ireland is more green. This looks burned out to Irish eyes. But it's just as holy and God created it all."

I moaned and he laughed. "Ah, that's all right, Ron. One of these days you'll realize you didn't create it so you're not to blame for how it looks. You're only responsible for taking care of it."

"Liam," I asked, "am I going to hear this Irish-Catholic recovery philosophy on every hole?"

"Ron," he said, "not only at every hole but in every sentence. Whether you pay attention is another matter, of course. You've still got so much shit in your ears." Then he laughed like his observations were the funniest thing going. Looking at me, being with me, sure seemed to amuse him.

We were standing at the open trunk of his car pulling out the bags of clubs. He and Andy nearly undressed and then redressed with golf shoes, sweaters and hats. Kevin and I were wearing jeans and tennis shoes. Kevin asked Liam: "Can Ron and I play in jeans?" Liam said "Yes. It's past the official season so there's no dress code." Liam looked at Andy's filthy canvas hat and said: "Oh, but Andy, you can't be wearing that. It's not right for you." He reached into the back of the trunk and brought out a tartan plaid cap and handed it to Andy. "Now, wear this. It suits you and your blond hair better." Andy took the cap with a huge grin and put it on. He started blushing.

I said: "Liam, don't you have hats for Kevin or me?"

"Ron," he said, "You don't automatically get something just because someone else does."

"Oh, I see. So Andy's the priest boy today. Be careful, Andy. It's just not Greeks bearing gifts that are dangerous."

"Ron," Liam said. "Not all presents are vipers either."

I stopped talking, grabbed my bag and walked to a golf cart. Liam said: "Andy and I will ride together and start off first. That way the two of you won't slow down play. We'll see you on the greens, though. There probably won't be any other golfers coming up behind you, but be mindful in case there are."

Andy and Liam took off first and hit their balls like they knew what they were doing. Kevin hit his ball like he mostly knew what he was doing. I hit mine with the force of the guy who put the ice-pick in Trotsky's head, but my ball glided about six inches while the dirt went about forty feet. I teed up another one, and it went about one hundred feet. I apologized to Kevin and he said: "Hey, no problem, man." Liam and Andy were laughing so hard I thought they'd fall out of their cart. Being the amusement of others in sports games always pisses me off. Liam shouted: "We'll see you at the beginning of the next hole." He and Andy then drove off.

Kevin was very patient with me, and by the end of the hole I pretty much was hitting the ball and not reconfiguring the contour of the course. When we met up with Liam and Andy, Liam said to me: "Have you thought much about your mother?"

I said: "Why would I do that? I'm supposed to be playing golf."

He said: "Maybe your game would be better if you did one or

the other but not both."

I said: "I wasn't thinking about her!"

He said: "Well, you weren't thinking about golf, either."

He was right. I don't know what I was thinking about, but it wasn't golf. I was just miserable.

He and Andy teed off again, Liam with a great whooping laugh and Andy with his priest-boy hat on. They got into their cart like laughing champions and watched while Kevin and I teed off. Kevin's went far but high. Andy said: "Kevin, you're not supposed to put the ball into orbit." I hit more dirt than ball and Liam said: "Ron, stop digging graves and join the living." They took off. Kevin drove to his ball while I walked the few feet to mine.

"Okay," I said to myself. "Play golf. Be one with the ball." I thought of all the yoga-Zen-one-with-the-universe stuff I had ever learned or heard. I looked at the ball and said: "You're not going to get the best of me." I hit it, and it went another three feet. Maybe I wasn't digging graves, but I was making deep enough holes to put full grown plants into. Kevin drove back and said: "Don't move your head. You keep moving your head."

So I tried it again and did not move my head. This time, the ball went straight and far. I tried to figure out what I had done right. Kevin said: "Hey, that's it, man. You got it going." Maybe the message of the "one with the universe" stuff was simply to pay attention to what I was doing.

At the next hole Liam said: "Better, Ron, but who are you hitting when you hit the ball?"

I said: "What is that supposed to mean? I'm hitting the ball."

"Well, then, hit the ball. Don't be hitting your teachers, parents or therapists," he said. Andy giggled and said something to Liam who laughed.

I said: "What did you say, Andy?" Andy said: "I'm not telling, because you'll hit me next!"

Liam said: "He said you're hitting Brand, which may not be a bad thing, but he's not here with us today. So be with us and nowhere else for a while."

The priest and the priest-boy took off again as well as they did before. Kevin did better and I didn't. I was thinking about all kinds of stuff. "Keep your head down," Kevin said again. He may as well have asked me how to make an atomic bomb. It was just something I didn't know how to do. I started to get angry and Kevin said: "Don't worry. Don't hurry. No one is behind us."

Maybe no one was behind us, but there was something in me. I started to get so angry. I was angry at everything: Liam for laughing; Andy for being good and being the priest-boy of the day; Kevin for his acceptance and calm. I just wanted to get fucked up, and I couldn't.

I looked around the course. It was autumn in the South. There were no great tall oaks. There were no bright maples. There was no scarlet sumac. But there were pines, some thin and many tall. The grass was still green. It was now humid and nearly hot. The sun was all ill-defined roundness of yellow covered by a haze. I was sweating but probably more from inner turmoil than from outside temperature. I didn't know how to feel about all this. Liam's lines, Andy's apparent happiness, and Kevin just being himself were driving me crazy.

"Okay," I said to myself. "Try some George Harrison." So I

kept reciting to myself: "Be here now. Be here now. Be here now." I was nowhere else. I could be noplace else. I could not think myself to another spot. I did not have super powers and knew that I couldn't get them by wishing, which was a frequent fantasy of mine when I was younger. I walked up to the ball and said to it: "You and I are here together. Liam, Kevin and Andy are here with us. They are being who they are. I need to be who I am." Then I thought again: "Be here now. Be here now." For a moment, just a moment, I let go of what I had been wrapping myself in and thought about this moment only. And in this moment, all I had to do was hit the ball, not Brand, not my parents. The ball was just a ball. All I had to do to hit it was to realize that. Which I did.

Kevin said: "Great shot, man!," to which I said: "Huh? Where is it?" I had kept my head down and was still looking at the ground. He said: "I saw it. Climb in. This time we'll drive to it."

At the beginning of the next hole, Liam said: "Ron, you must be getting religion! Either that or you've got a magic ball!"

"Liam," I said, "I hate priests, so shut up." Andy and Kevin looked upset at that, even shocked. Andy looked as though he were going to say something in Liam's defense. Liam loudly laughed again and said: "I know you do! That's a sign of your great spirituality! On to the next hole."

I was getting sick of his beginning-of-the-hole one-liners, but I was getting hooked on them also. How was my hatred of priests related to being spiritual? I would have thought it was the opposite. Andy's delight in being priest-boy of the day was disgusting. Kevin's calm was the professional calm of the doctor, waiting for someone to go through misery so that the professional could take credit, get on with his own life, or simply feel superior. Well, I said to myself, he needs to lose weight. And Andy needs to lose that smile. And Liam needs to lose his joy and, most importantly, his one-liners. I was so angry. I was mad at myself for hitting dirt, for not being graceful, for not being charming and, probably most importantly, for being so miserable.

I said: "Liam, how about explaining these Catholic recovery cryptic messages. I'm getting a little bored with the games of golf and 'meaning.'" Liam smiled and said: "Oh, Ron, you are so impatient. You can't even enjoy being here."

"Enjoy?" I said. "Enjoy what? Your puzzles? My feet are wet and cold. I feel like I'm in a trunk. I'm cold, wet and miserable."

He was bending over his tee, placing his ball on top and smiling. I got so angry when he smiled. I wished I had driven my own car so I could leave, but even if I had and did, I didn't know how to get back without him. "Ron," he said, "one last sentence, then, to think about as we finish: pain is inevitable while misery is chosen."

It was like he slapped me. I couldn't move I was so shocked. I had thought the misery was forced upon me. I didn't realize until he said that clear sentence that I had not dealt with my pain at all except to make myself miserable and more miserable. I started to say something, but he was starting to swing. Andy looked at me, shook his head back and forth and put his finger to his lips. I didn't say anything. I watched Andy tee off and then Kevin. After he hit the ball, Kevin said: "You okay, man?"

I said: "Yeah, I think. Maybe. I don't know." I put my ball on the tee and it fell off. I put it back on. The three of them were looking at me quietly, patiently. I hated that. But I stood over the ball, kept my eyes on it, swung and hit it. This time I hit more of the ball than the dirt. I climbed in the cart with Kevin, who drove us on the path of grass in the foggy, rainy, thick Georgia pines to the spots where we would each make our next stroke. Was it Liam who said "it's not the destination, it's the journey" or was it some ersatz sixties leftover song-lyric philosophy? Maybe it was someone who is preserved more in *Bartlett's* than in the conscious culture. I couldn't remember. But Liam stopped his thoughts-for-a-day and just started saying things like "good shot," or he simply laughed, which was both better and worse than the calendar sheet philosophy.

It started raining real rain, which felt just as cold to me as fall Michigan rain. Neither Kevin nor I said anything about going in. He and I sat in our cart nearly hugging each other to get protection from the rain, while Andy the priest-boy and Liam stood in the rain. Andy stood there, grinning then giggling, as Liam kept trying to wipe the rain out of his eyes. "Well, lads," he said, "what do you say we go to the clubhouse and sit by the fire while we wait for this fog to lift?"

"Fog?" Kevin said.

"Oh, Kevin," said Liam. "I keep forgetting you're from California, where everything is always so pleasant."

"Liam," said Kevin, "in California, this is called winter."

"Kevin," Liam said, rolling the r's with both care and gusto, and some exaggeration, "it's all relative, isn't it?"

We drove back to the clubhouse, liberated some towels from the men's locker room and then sat by the fire. Liam offered us cigars, which Kevin and I accepted but which Andy turned down. As we smoked, Andy took his priest-boy hat off his head and put it over his mouth.

"Jeez, Andy," I said, "not only did you have to wear the priest-boy hat, now you've got to breathe through it? Talk about sucking up."

"It's the smoke from the cigars," Andy said. "I hate it."

"But you could smoke crack without a problem, right?" I said.

"Oh, leave the boy alone," said Liam, "your logic will kill us all. Have some faith that he's doing the right thing."

"I'm still waiting for the book on that," I said, "and don't tell me it's the Bible."

Kevin said: "Ron, he's Catholic, I don't think they read the Bible. At least not in Georgia."

We all laughed at that. Liam said: "Oh, Kevin, Ron's going to lead you straight to hell!"

We sat for a long while saying nothing. After a while, Kevin quizzed Liam on treatment topics and Andy kept up his dramatic anti-smoking show. Liam said: "It's time to go" so he and Andy got undressed and redressed again, this time in the dry locker room.

As we got close to the car, I said: "I want to sit behind you, Liam, so I've got some leg room. Let priest-boy sit up front with you." Liam just smiled and Andy touched his hat.

As we drove back, the rain cut back to a drizzle, the kind where you set your wipers to go across the windshield every so often instead of constantly. It was nearly dusk, and with the clouds and drizzle it reminded me of a Michigan November. When Liam turned his headlights on, the rear view mirror lit up and so did dim reading lights in the back seat. They had an orange tinge, sort of like the fire at the golf clubhouse.

Kevin started quizzing Liam again about treatment. Finally, he said the question he obviously had been waiting to ask all day: "Liam, how long do you think I'll be here?"

Keeping his eyes on the road, Liam said: "Oh, Kevin, not real long. You've got a supportive wife, you were caught very early in your disease, and you've got a great attitude about getting healthy."

I was so afraid to ask the same question, but I wanted the same answer, so I asked him: "Liam, what about me?

Liam took his eyes off the road and looked at me through the orange-lit, rear-view mirror. He laughed and nearly roared when he said: "Ron, you're going to be here a long, long time!" And then Andy and Kevin laughed with him. When I heard that, I was scared, but I also was beginning to feel like I belonged.

Why Are They So Mean To Him?

After I had been in treatment a few weeks, Christina, a friend from college days, sent me Xeroxed photos of she, I, and other friends taken while we were in college. She had put these together in a homemade book with bright ribbon binding the edges. The cover was a copy of something Yoko Ono had written in her book Grapefruit, which Chris and I love. We were Yoko defenders. Chris always said that Yoko didn't break up the Beatles. Instead, she said, the Beatles broke up the Beatles. In some ways Chris was like Yoko, an unrealized and unappreciated artist. In other ways she was very different.

Chris was so beautiful people would stop on the street to look at her. More than once a photographer asked to take her picture for the sheer joy of doing it. One of them took a head shot and produced a poster. Chris' hair was jet black, her eyes were as dark but glittered with fantastic light. The poster was a profile with nothing but her hair and eyes developed. I wish I had it.

I was thrilled to get something from her. I had loved her so much in college and had been so afraid to love her. I was terrified by any sexual thoughts and, besides, I had no idea how to have a girlfriend or any relationship besides that of an intellectual cocksman. On top of that, she and her boyfriend had been going together since seventh grade. I had no idea how to love someone. All I knew was how to be a charming, cocky, know-it-all.

We all charmed each other. We lived together in a rented house in the poor part of town so that we could be closer to the "workers."

Phil, another unrealized artist and friend of mine since junior high school, also lived with us. College for us was, in a phrase of the times, mystical and magical. We fit the era and the era fit us. We all felt so special. Chris' boyfriend, Chato, had been editor of the school paper but was removed by the administration for a headline he wrote when Art Linkletter's daughter died while on LSD. She had jumped to her death from a high window. Chato's main headline was simple enough: "Art Linkletter's Daughter Dies." It was the "kicker headline" over the main one which led to his removal: "Kids Do The Darndest Things."

His punishment motivated Chris and I to run for student government office. She became student body "secretary," and I became student body "president." We wound up in such controversy after a while that we, too, were removed from our positions. It was time to graduate anyway. Chris, Chato and Phil all moved to a house on Lake Michigan with others who were much more drug-friendly and literate than I. I went to law school. We all kept in touch with each other over the years, but we built separate lives. And, of course, my personal life was kept so secret that even I hardly knew it existed.

Initially, I was glad to get the photos Chris sent me. They were pictures of us at my parents' house, which was on a lake. Phil, Chato and I all wore Speedos, as though we were on a swim team or vacationing in Europe as opposed to being at a small lake in southern Michigan.

I took the photos to my counselor Kathy, who was in college at about the same time as we were. She had lived through "The Revolution," knew the music, the issues, the assumptions, the conceits and the ignorance. As we looked at the photos in her office, I told her who Chris, Chato and Phil were. I kept talking about Chris' beauty. Kathy quietly asked: "Is she still so beautiful?"

I said: "Well, like me, she's gained a few pounds. Her hair isn't jet black now. The black is the color of old coal and it's mixed with silver the color of new stainless steel."

Kathy said: "You're telling me what she looks like. I want to know if she's still beautiful." I didn't get what she meant. I was trying to say she was still beautiful. Kathy waited silently, smiling. Then she said: "I wonder if your gift for description doesn't get in the way of your feelings. Do you always have to create a description for something before you can feel it?"

I couldn't say anything and I started to cry. Kathy sat there, saying nothing, not moving. I felt ashamed of crying, but I couldn't help it. The crying became worse, nearly hysterical. After a while, I said: "I don't know what's wrong with me. This just comes over me sometimes."

Kathy asked: "You don't have any idea why you cry like that?"

I got control of myself enough to say: "No. I don't."

Kathy looked through the photos again as I gained more control of myself. She pointed at a picture of me standing at the end of a dock, leaning on a water ski, cocky and confident looking, gazing across the lake as though I could see the future. She said: "Why are you so mean to this guy?"

I had no idea what she meant. "What?" She repeated herself: "Why are you so mean to this guy?" I started crying again. I sobbed. "I have no idea what you are talking about. I was never mean to myself."

She said: "Aren't you being mean now?" The sobbing and crying were verging on hysteria. I tried to control myself. I smiled and said: "I'm sorry. I don't know how you put up with this from patients."

Kathy said: "Don't worry about being nice to me. I know how to be nice to me. Be nice to yourself." She pointed at the photo again and said: "Just tell me why you are so mean to this guy."

I became hysterical. I didn't know what she meant, but I knew that what she said was true. Mean to me? Why not be mean to me? It's the best thing I learned. No one could be meaner to me. If I could survive my concept of meanness, then I could survive anything.

After a few minutes, I said: "A few years ago, I was at a friend's birthday party. A very drunk and obnoxious old man came up to me and said: 'Are you Charlie Fabian's son?' I said: 'Yes. I'm the youngest. Number five in a series of five.' That guy then said: 'Are you as mean as he was?' I said: 'I hope not.' He then said, with great admiration, as though he were talking about Neil Armstrong or some great hero: 'He was the meanest son-of-a-bitch I ever met. You must be, too, to be his son and still alive.'"

Kathy waited a moment and said: "It must have been horrible growing up like that."

I wiped my eyes and nose with my cuff and said: "Well, it was like being raised in a terrorist camp, but the training was so complete. I can handle almost anything."

Kathy said: "Yet, still, you're here. Maybe there was something you didn't want to handle."

I said nothing. She said: "I've got a group. Make sure you come back tomorrow to talk."

I reached for the photos. She said: "Let me keep these for tonight."

I wondered why she wanted them and was a little bothered by her keeping them, but I shrugged and said: "okay."

I walked back to the dome feeling like I did after each car accident I had: Sad, numb and operating on automatic with my mind on the past. If I had done just something different; If I had left Michigan after college, after law school, when I was thirty; If I hadn't mixed alcohol with pills; If I had only hung out with educated people. I felt like I did in the jail cell. I felt like I was dying.

I didn't talk to anyone through dinner. After dinner, I just said: "I need to use the phone."

Even though we weren't supposed to, I took the telephone out on the apartment patio and closed the glass door. It was hot and muggy. The night noises were full of insects. The smells were pine mixed with barbeque. Even though I felt miserable, I laughed at myself and said: "Well, that's the smell of Georgia."

I called friends at home, crying while talking with each one of them, asking: "Who would I have been without abuse? Who was I meant to be?" Each friend was tolerant, loving and helpless. Each said: "You are a good person." I said: "No, no I'm not."

I called my sister Beverly. I got hysterical. I kept asking the same questions. I started talking about dying and about how there was no reason to live. I would never have a life. No one would ever love me. I would never earn a living again. My reputation was gone. My income was gone. I needed to start all over again and the only way to do that was to die and then be reborn. Bev kept trying to be rational. She examined each thought and feeling as I used to when I had clients, when I was somebody. I kept objecting.

She finally raised her voice: "Shut up! Listen!" Hearing Beverly use the voice of command while saying "shut up" was, for me, like hearing Mother Theresa say: "You motherfucker!"

I listened. She continued. "You are who you are. You will be what you will be. You are lonely, scared and feeling sorry for yourself. Just stop it!" I stopped sobbing and started listening.

She said: "Give this a chance. But even if you run away, even if you go to prison, I will always love you. You will always have a place with me."

I don't know how she knew, but that was one of the things my fear was feeding on: "You have no place to go." Hearing her say that wasn't true did quiet me.

She said: "Go sit and talk with some of the guys in the dome. Don't isolate. Talk to Cliff and Kathy tomorrow.

I said: "okay," and started to hang up. She said: "Ron?" I said: "Yeah?" "I love you. Never forget that."

I started crying again. I said: "I never said this to you before, but I love you too."

She said: "I know. And it's nice to hear."

I hung up the phone and walked back into the apartment. The nice southern boy was sitting in the living room. He said: "How you doing, man?"

I said: "okay. But I'm sick and tired of living in his movie of mine."

He said: "The great thing is that it is your movie. It's your story. Nobody else's." He said those short sentences with such a sincere drawl that it sounded like the Sermon on the Mount.

I looked at him, smiled, and asked: "Where's Eddy?"

He said: "On the deck smoking, waiting for you."

The southern boy and I went outside, said nothing and sat down. Eddy was there with about six other guys, all smoking cigars or cigarettes. I don't remember what they were talking about, but they were laughing. After a few minutes Eddy said: "You okay, man?"

I said: "I guess. Better than I was."

Eddy said: "That's good."

He and the other guys kept smoking, talking and laughing. They started telling stories about how to figure out each counselor and how to give each what they wanted. Brand had been sitting there. He looked at me and said: "You must have Cliff figured out."

I said: "Why would you say that?"

He said: "Because he likes you."

I laughed. That was so absurd to say. I had no idea if Cliff liked me or if it even mattered.

"All I can tell you, Brand, is that I answer his questions honestly. I cry in front of him. I tell him I'm ashamed of the things I've done. I don't know how this would make him like me."

Brand grinned at me like I was a used car salesman, telling him that the engine noise was nothing and that flat tires were normal.

"Brand," I said, "I can tell you're not going to believe this, but I'll tell you anyway. I have been so miserable that I wanted to die. So miserable that I thought death was the only way out of the misery. I have never felt safe. I have used whatever talents I have to keep myself from being hurt. That closed me off from life and love."

I stopped talking and looked at my feet. All the guys were silent, looking at me as though they expected me to say more.

I raised my head, looked at him in the eyes and smiled: "I used to think there was a garden, somewhere, where I would smell ancient flowers with scents that would protect me from gloom, flowers with such perfect perfume that I would become so intoxicated that I'd never need to leave that garden. I never found that garden, and I got so angry. I kept wishing for someone to take me away."

No one was moving. Brand was gritting his teeth. His face was turning red. The rest of the guys were still looking directly at me. I took this for permission to go on.

"I got so angry I wanted to throw bombs, not caring where they'd land or what damage they'd do, whether to me or to others. When I went out on the street, there was such hassle for me. No one and nothing filled my desire. I retreated to a garden of fantasy constructed not with flowers and nature but with vodka and Vicodin. My garden became a continuous nightmare. Even when I stood in the sun, I felt as though I were in a dark box."

The looks on the faces of the other guys were such that I knew I had touched on a common theme, a common feeling.

I said: "Now I have the tiniest bit of hope that I don't have to be mean to myself anymore; that there is the slightest chance that I might have some kind of life. But, if it ends here, then it ends here."

Brand said: "You're such a crybaby."

Some of the other guys started to say something but Eddy's voice was first: "That's not fair, Brand."

I said: "No, it's not, but it's true. I am a crybaby. At least right now. Who knows how long I'll cry. I don't even know what I'm crying about or what for. I figure I've got almost fifty years of tears stored up inside of me. But at least I am having a feeling, whatever it is."

I looked at Eddy: "And he's not fair."

Then I looked at Brand and said: "It doesn't matter to me if you're fair or if life is fair. I'd like life to be fair to all of us. I used to worry so much about fairness. I did righteous indignation better than anyone I know. But I'm beginning to think that if fairness remains a goal, I'll never have peace of mind. And if I worry about what's fair, then I'm still playing God. And I sure wasn't very good at that."

I kept looking at Brand. "If Cliff likes me, great. But I'm not here for him to like me. I'm here for him to help me get a life."

Brand said: "You're just queer for him!"

I said: "Brand, maybe I am. I don't know."

I stopped talking. No one said anything for a while. The southern boy looked at me and said: "Man, if I ever need a lawyer I'm going to call you."

I smiled at him and said: "Well, it's yet to be determined if I'll be allowed to practice law."

Brand glared at the southern boy and said: "That's all bullshit, man. He's all bullshit."

Eddy laughed and so did I. Eddy said: "That's what being a lawyer is all about!"

I remembered my earlier conversation with Kathy and said: "Brand, this is going to sound cryptic, but Yoko didn't break up the Beatles, the Beatles broke up the Beatles. And no one has ever been meaner to me than me. You're wasting your time trying."

Eddy laughed again. "Stop with the Beatles shit, man. Let's go to bed."

Der Romp und Schtomp

It's actually called "Romp and Stomp," but a lot of the new patients think that it's run by a Nazi, and the older ones see that as true: a recovery Nazi. The older patients use their ersatz, WWII movie accents just to unnerve those who have not yet received their initiation.

It's a weekly ritual welcoming new patients and saying goodbye to those who have successfully completed treatment. It always takes place in the auditorium on Thursday and immediately precedes an AA meeting. The auditorium is a windowless room in the middle of the recovery building. It has two sets of very noisy double doors on opposite walls and the chairs are all neatly arranged in rows. All current patients are required to attend. The members of each "dome" are supposed to sit with each other. It is one of the high points of the week, because it is the one group session where you can be reasonably certain that you will not have to talk, confess, divulge or take part in something unless you want to. This is a group where you can sit against the wall or cast your eyes to the floor without your behavior being commented upon. It's like sleeping in on snow days or Saturdays. It's the one group you do want to get involved with, because someone else is going to get it no matter what!

Karen, a director of the recovery center, whose addicted drug of choice was Demerol, runs the show. The routine is the same. She starts off by questioning: "Who's new here?" and the response is invariably "Rich people!" Then she says "Who's leaving?" and the response is "Poor people!" She makes faces at this. She is a wonderfully talented, natural comedienne. She doesn't have just one liners, she has a whole shtick. Her face moves. Her body moves. She is a big woman, but she is like a combination of Martha Raye and Lucille Ball. If you've never seen *Big Broadcast of 1938*, go rent it. Martha Raye is this very funny woman and an incredible dancer. She may be the person the word "hoofer" was first used for. Karen is the same way. A big person but lithe and incredibly fast. She can go from the front of the auditorium to the back faster than your eye. The old timers watch for this. They watch for the smart ass who makes a comment thinking Karen won't catch it or, if she does, one she will let go. Nothing goes by her. She catches all comments and some she simply deals with by using her face. She has more expressive looks than all of the faces in the room put together. Her face is rubbery, like Lucille Ball's, and she can be petulant. She communicates with her entire body. She commands attention. She is also smart. She knows when to back off someone who is about to collapse, and she knows when to drill into someone who needs one more layer of denial torn away.

She starts off with a contest: "Who will announce the five things?" Before new people can even figure out what this means, older patients are screaming the names of various other patients: "Jeff! He's finally learned how to talk!" "Phillip!! You can hardly hear him breathe!" "Alice!!!! She's not so brain dead anymore!" All in reference to Jeff, who hasn't said a word since the day he came in; Phillip who has smoked so much dope and crack cocaine that he, at age 35, breathes like a lifetime asbestos miner; and Alice, who was so brain dead when she came in you practically had to pin her name on her shirt so she'd remember who she was.

Though all of us have our tragedies, the female alcoholics seem the worse. There is a medical phenomena, actually a condition, called "Wet Brain," which comes from so much drinking that the person can't process information in real time. You've seen people like this, but usually after there is no potential for recovery. You've seen them walking down the street, hanging out at the post office, or picking up cans. This is the person for whom you extend the unseen and quiet courtesy of touching your automatic door lock when you are stopped at a light and she is carrying her garbage bag of pop cans. It's the same person who has a bundle of newspaper in one hand, an old Windex bottle filled with God-knows-what in the other, and a hideous smile when you are at that same light praying that it turns green before he gets to your windshield. This is the same person you close your eyes and pray: "Dear God, please don't let them see me," just like a two year old making the real world disappear by closing your eyes. Karen welcomes this person, kids them, makes fun of them, breaks them down with humor and very rough grace on the mere possibility that they can be restored. The fact that some insurance company, rich relative or trust fund is paying the initial bill doesn't hurt either.

After the names are shouted, Karen picks some druggie, which is what we all are, or some criminal, which is what we all are, to announce the five things. That person comes up out of the group to the front with a huge grin. By the time a person has been chosen, he or she has gone through so much treatment, paranoia, anger, angst, guilt and shame that being chosen by Karen is a momentary reprieve from these negative feelings. "Finally," the patient is silently saying, "finally, Karen likes me." In actual fact, of course, Karen neither likes nor dislikes. Today she is doing treatment. There was some reason to pick that person to say the five things. Either they were resistant to treatment or they were too compliant. Either they were too angry or not angry enough. The balance is constantly being sought. Karen is a master of intuitive manipulation. If she ran the White House, there would be no bozos on board. She is like a lie detector of the soul. Of course, it helps that she had read the detailed thirty-page bio-chemical-social history form each patient spends hours filling out for the staff.

The crowd is now chanting the name of the person saying the Five Things: "Alice, Alice, Alice," they shout. Alice stands next to Karen with a huge grin on her face. She now gets to show her stuff. She gets to show why men liked her so much, and being sober, she says to herself, won't detract one bit from that attraction. If she actually shows this conceit, Karen will use it in group next time: "Alice, I can't believe, after all this treatment, you still act like a whore in front of a bunch of addicted men. Men are as much your drug as cocaine! Get some respect for yourself. You're not going to get it from them!" This is delivered in a staccato, machine gun blast style. She could have said: "The cake's done" and everyone in earshot, and that would be a lot of people, would still stop and think. Having your innermost secrets delivered to the world leaves no retreat. You either deal with it or run back to the self-pity burrow that got you here.

Alice, or Phillip or whomever, is now grinning and holding up one hand in a fist. Then one finger is extended: "One!" Everyone then says: "One!" The chorus is a roar loud enough to scare a lion. "What's your name?" The roar then says: "Name!" "Two" "Two" is the shout-back. "Where did you used to live?" The "used to live" is emphasized by the chorus. Because now you live with us and you have no idea when you're going home. For many patients there is no home. What was home will be split by divorces filed while they are in treatment, loss of home due to no income, and the old-fashioned type of divorce that lawyers hate: simple abandonment. Honey, I've moved on. "Used to live" is underlined because it is so painful. "There's no place like home" new patients sing to themselves for reassurance. "There is no home" old patients chant.

"Three!" And the announcement of this number triggers hysteria. It is the question which gets the most response and the patients who can stand are on their feet. "Three!" comes the chorus response, not unlike the spectators at a bullfight who can see from their special perspective what the bull cannot: You are about to get gored. "What did you used to do?" As soon as that question is answered, the very second the profession or lack of it is known, then comes question four, which is the question, the only question, with the only answer which really matters or interests: Four is "What's your drug of choice?". But before the question can even get out, the old patients are screaming the answer the second the job or former job is known.

If the person says: "Anesthesiologist," then the screams are all the same. This is an easy one. There is only one drug these guys take. They are one of the few who can get it, since it is so tightly regulated. It is reported to be 1000 times, that is one thousand times, more powerful than morphine. It's effects are fairly short-term, so a cranked up gas-passer can get high, get un-high, see a patient, see his wife, go home, take some in bed ("honey, I've got a headache. I'm going to go to bed early") and lie there wishing only he could turn up the volume on a song only he can hear. What? Forget the volume, the colors are too bright to have sound with them. What? Pass out time.

If some poor new soul says "attorney," there is complete derision. It's easy to hate lawyers, even more so in treatment because the medical people know the lawyers are going to hear their sins about how people died for the doctors' drugs. The drugs of choice of lawyers are easy to guess too. There are only two drugs for them. If they could write prescriptions, *Oh my God!* because they get so screwed up, and incredibly creative, on the few drugs they can easily get. But the Latin they know is about rights, suppression of rights, or how to speak a language more dead than the doctors' patients. Plus, they don't have prescription pads. Of course, if they can compromise a doctor, maybe by forgiving an unpaid divorce bill, or by introducing some unlucky doctor to an even unluckier quasi-legal secretary in a dimly lit, crusty bar, then the sky is the limit. But without that kind of printing press, and not knowing enough medical Latin to actually forge a prescription, the lawyers have to content themselves with the country club acceptables: discrete and very expensive cocaine ("Yes, I've had this cold for a very long time, Mrs. Smith") or the grape itself: beer, wine and liquor. Usually vodka because everyone believes it doesn't smell. When you see a lawyer with whiskey, watch out. He doesn't care who knows he drinks and he doesn't care to whom he's mean. He's written off the world and he's dying to taste living flesh. A lawyer with a nose burned out by cocaine who is looking for the best free rhinoplasty surgeon is much more kind.

Nurses are harder to guess. Since they often dispense nearly all drugs, they have access to nearly all drugs. Once they taste Hydrocodone, they never come back. It's such a popular drug, with so many brand names, that there really isn't much excitement over guessing which version of it they take. Besides, a drug camp like this one unconsciously reinforces the snobbery and placement of the outside world. Arrogant surgeons on top and nurses on the bottom, even in the addict world.

The arrogance of surgeons shines out even as they introduce themselves, but their drugs don't shine. Their drugs are done in top secret so as to keep their demigod status intact. More often, crack cocaine, the drug of losers and beer bottle collectors, is the drug of high and mighty surgeons. Even they cannot escape its instant Jesus high and its incredible cheapness. It is with the surgeons most especially that the protector demon, denial, shows its head and power. "What, me, an addict?" says the surgeon. "I'm only here to please my partners because, for some weird reason, the random urine test we all have to take came back positive. I'm sure it was because of the incompetent med tech, but I said I'd come for a four-day evaluation."

"Four days!" We all go into hysterics. This is so funny to us as we sit rompin' and stompin'. Andy is nearly on his knees with laughter and if I had soda pop in my mouth it would be coming out my nose. "Four days? More like four years!" yells the former head of surgery of a famous big city hospital. He has been here nine months following a four-day evaluation. The "four-day evaluation" here at drug camp is like the famous "three-hour tour." Once you step on board, you don't get off until God allows it. God in this case is usually Karen.

There are occasionally celebrities among us. One time we had a sports hero who was simply huge. When he announced what he did, the rest of us for once were silent. No one could immediately assign a drug to him. I then shouted that his drug was "Milk!" and got a huge laugh. The celebrities don't last long. They are not catered to, and having to do their own laundry and cooking is beyond them. One of them did no laundry and, instead, bought new clothes the entire time he was in treatment. He never washed anything. When he left, he left his wardrobe behind. But he was so large that no one could wear anything. Andy took one of his sweaters but he had to wrap it around himself to wear it.

There are the non-professionals who come to treatment also. Usually they are corporate executives who really have lived life in the fast lane, their wives, or true rich kids. Some of these kids are so rich that their parents fly them down in their private jets, drop them off, kiss them goodbye with a lecture to "be good," turn around and go home. Call me when you're well. Other such parents spend a lot of time being involved in the therapy trying to help their child. Either way, the kids don't care. All they want is to use again. Most of the rich kids simply do not get into this. They are still bullet-proof, invulnerable and only here to please the folks, get the trust fund or stay out of jail. The disease loves their belief that they are invulnerable. The more they believe that, the more the disease can get them to use. They count down the days until they can leave. They take the mechanics of manipulation whining to levels unimaginable by anyone who is not a rich kid. They are easy to spot. No one would wear their clothes. They are dirty, ratty, full of holes and stains. They wear, of course, work boots as if to show their solidarity with a world which they have heard about vaguely, somewhere. But these work boots usually cost more than a normal workers' weekly wages. If they wear glasses, they are invariably incredibly ugly eyepieces, but very, very expensive. The uglier the better. The smellier the better. "See," they say, "can't you tell I am regular?" Their whines are as irritating as fingernails on a chalk board. These kids make tense guitar strings twang the second their lips start to move. Their great goal is life is to learn to talk without saying "I, me, mine" within the first dozen words of a conversation, but once they get beyond the weather and "cool, man," you might as well be teaching them Sanskrit. Karen, for some reason, usually leaves them alone at Romp and Stomp. She says the worst patients are professional athletes, lawyers and rich kids. Maybe she writes the kids off at the start. Who knows. Very few finish treatment. Those who do actually go into other recovery centers.

One of the executives was very scared during his time at Romp and Stomp. In answer to the "What did you used to do?" question, he stuttered that he owned a furniture manufacturing company. As soon as Andy and I heard that, we yelled out that his drug of choice was "Lemon Pledge!" He looked at us as if to say: "You mean, you can get high from that too?"

There is a ruthlessness and purpose to all this. It takes ruthlessness to get through the protective walls set up by the Disease. The worst ones, the absolute worst ones, the ones who suffer quick visible brain damage and who exist in a living hell, are the driller dentists. When a dentist announces his or her occupation the only drug of choice yelled out is "Nitrous!" over and over and over again by the expert other professional addicts. The nitrous invades the gentle yielding soft flesh of the brain and turns it into silly putty. The invisible gas takes up residence between the synapses, between the neurons, to keep those essential connections from being made so that when one part of the brain says: "Fire!" the other part is asleep, dreaming in some old Coleridge Xanadu or some more modern Lucy in the Sky, but dreaming away and refusing to fire just like an old wet spark plug with rust on it. Still there, but worthless. Just like with some of those rusty spark plugs when there is more rust than metal and nothing left once the rust is scraped away, so is the brain of the dentist.

One time one of them locked himself in his examination room, and then put bungee cords from the door handles to permanent brackets on the opposite walls so no one could get in. He then lashed together two tanks to avoid the automatic, safeguard shut-off valves so he could suck the gas for twelve hours. He was so happy in that chair, sailing away like Kubla Kahn in a boat on a river with Lucy. But then, his suspicious wife, who thought he was having an affair with the tooth cleaner in that chair, broke down the door with an axe only to find him alone, humming some indecipherable song that only a gas addict could hear. Even with his new and much lower IQ, he is still mad at her. "Four!" It is now anti-climatic. We only listen to see if our drug choices were right. But we already know what they are and, if we're wrong, it will give us something to talk about in the lounge.

Then, finally, "Five." This one still gives some amusement. "Where you do live now?" Where indeed? Some insane asylum for the rich. That's where. As one of the counselors so lovingly said in his foreign accent: "Sixty years ago they would have stripped you down, hosed you off, locked you up and thrown away the key." Some progress. Now they charge us a fortune, tell us to "get over it, do your own cooking, and make your bed daily." The new ones are still standing at this point and their domemates are whispering what to say, which is their apartment number. Some get it and some don't. I didn't. When Karen then individually asked me "Where do you live now?" all I could say was: "With these gentlemen" while pointing at the members of my community. She looked at me and said: "If you think these are gentlemen, you really are fucked up."

Skit Night

We were required to have fun. This was actually hard for lots of us because there were requirements under the requirement: all fun had to be in the company of others and it had to be substance free. People like Andy, Pam and I simply fell back into our standard behaviors of sarcasm and dissecting others. This was funny to us, but it wasn't, in the eyes of staff, "fun." They called it "diversion" and "avoidance" when we talked about how another patient drooled for weeks after release from detox or kept walking into closed doors, apparently thinking they would automatically open. They said this was "default behavior" which we're supposed to shed while learning to be "real people."

Andy had this technique of making fun of someone by simply saying or whispering his name, which got the rest of us to laugh but which pushed the recipient to the point of murder. Andy intuitively knew who and how to pick. Andy especially liked picking on Tony. During Sunday Spiritual, the rest of us would lie on the floor in the dark room waiting for some connection to our individual Higher Powers. Andy, however, would wait for a lull in the sharing or the music and then stage-whisper "Tony," as though a malevolent ghost were calling him from the ether. Andy did this week after week so that we, like Pavlov's dogs, expected it. We could not, would not, be disappointed. Before Spiritual, some of us would say "Andy, leave Tony alone" and others would say "Andy, I think he's about ready to break." Andy, being the addict's addict, being unable to resist a laugh, no matter how evil, did not disappoint. He'd whisper "Tony," with the same effect as cold water dripping on soft stone. He was relentless, steady and purposeful. He knew he could bore a hole in Tony's soul just as water would in limestone. And he cared as much about Tony as the water did about the stone. Andy was into reactions and results.

The staff didn't like us using our default behaviors, which behaviors they believed had originally gotten us into trouble. We thought the same behavior was what had also allowed us to survive as long as we had. Learning to "have fun" without chemicals or corrosive behaviors was not easy.

Karen, who herself was the queen of caustic comments, scheduled a "skit night" every two months or so. There were about four weeks from the time she announced it to the night itself. I had only been there about a month and didn't know what was expected. After one "First Step," she said: "Some of you have heard this, but the newer patients haven't. We're going to have a "skit night," which she pronounced in the exaggerated southern manner as "skeeit ny-it."

She continued: "Each dome has to come up with some entertainment for the staff and the other patients. I call these 'skits.' You can call them what you want, but you will perform. These performances will take place here in the main auditorium. There are four rules: 1) everyone has to participate; 2) don't tell the other domes what you are planning; 3) be funny and; 4) have fun!" When she gave the rules, though, it was like listening to Alice's Queen. We never knew when she might add: "Off with his head!"

I had only been there about four weeks when she made this announcement, and I was very frightened of her.

The preparation in the domes was the same as a bunch of eighth graders getting ready for the homecoming parade. At first no one had any ideas. Then one or two of the class clowns would propose outrageous ideas. Andy wanted to have a farting contest. Tony wanted to re-do "Hamlet," placing it in a drug treatment center. One of the dentists, who used to be able to play the guitar but lost his ability when he was exchanging oxygen molecules with those of nitrous oxide, wanted to "get a band together and sing 'Louie Louie.'" He cried when his roommate reminded him he had lost his knowledge of the three simple chords of the song and he had sold his guitar to get dope. Someone made the Judy Garland/Mickey Rooney comment: "I've got a barn!" Most of the rest of us simply groaned.

Pam, though, really got into it. She and I become double agent spies, telling the other what we knew of the plans of the other domes. We heavily critiqued the embryonic plans of the others for any number of reasons but mostly because they simply weren't funny. I thought she should get the other women to dress up as hysterical historical female characters delivering their First Steps. "Imagine," I said, "Judy Garland giving her 'First Step,' or better yet, Marie Antoinette. 'Cake, I must have cake....'" Pam and I would laugh about the consequences of the cake obsession. "So then we all lost our heads!" We collapsed at our own cleverness. Then Pam said: "It would never work. Some of the women can't even remember their own names." She took the idea back to the women's dome and though they all thought it was a great idea, they wound up fighting over who would get to play Monica Lewinsky, which was the historical character they knew the best and most identified with.

Since I had "come out," the other guys in my dome thought that

I, as the only openly gay man, should organize our skit. Initially I refused, complaining about stereotypes and prejudice. A dentist from Memphis said: "C'mon, Ron," pronounced in the southern way "Raahn," "you must know all the great show tunes. You can come up with something." "Okay," I said, "You can be Judy Garland and I'll be Mickey Rooney. You give me a blow job during which I'll sing 'Yankee Doodle Dandy. How's that sound?" He rejected the idea and went to Cliff, who came to me wanting to know if I had "noticed my hostility." "Noticed it?" I said, "I've been living it for 49 years." True to type, though, I played coy for a couple of weeks and then proceeded to the planning.

We had too many egos to do something truly cohesive so I just said: "Let's do a revue. Brand, you have the least actual talent, so you get to be MC. We'll call you 'Dick Clark' and you'll get to present the rest of us as acts." Brand hadn't lost any of his default behavior and was extremely suspicious of anything I said. He started to look angry, but his roommate Michael said: "That's a great idea! Brand you can put on your church suit. You'll look great." Michael had been learning to manage Brand and the appeal to Brand's narcissism was irresistible. Everyone else liked the revue idea well enough, so over the next few weeks we'd talk about what each of us would do.

Tony really wanted to do "Hamlet," so I said: "okay. Rewrite the soliloquy from the perspective of an addict." Eddy refused to do anything because "I'm going to be out of here soon, man, and I've already done one. Karen can just get fucked." The rest of us were not willing to take on either Eddy or Karen so we simply moved on. The nice southern boy who had lent me his guitar when I first got out of detox, said: "I sing with my church choir, but I don't think well enough to sing right now, but I can still play a guitar all right." Billy said: "Great! You can play and I'll sing. Ron, write me a song!" I laughed and said: "I'll rewrite you one if I can play the lead guitar break." He and Southern Boy said: "okay!" Andy still refused to get involved unless he could fart, which all of us continued to veto.

The Professor said he would be a carrot. None of us understood what he meant "You see, Dr. Handle talks about the non-addictive qualities of carrots. You remember? You were at his lecture. At least your bodies were. You must remember that he said just because you liked carrots you were not obsessed with them. I will prove him wrong. I will paint myself with orange paint, dye my hair green and prove in an intellectual discourse that carrots are addictive and destructive. You must have faith. I will be brilliant."

Billy kept bugging me for a song. I said: "Leave me alone. I'll get you one." I turned over every song I knew in my head. The Beatles were simply too hard. Too many chord changes. Too much melody. You really had to be good to do their stuff. Motown was out because we simply didn't have a beat. Dylan kept coming into my head. At night, I started re-writing the lyrics to "All Along the Watchtower." The guitar was simple and Southern Boy could handle that. It also gave me an excuse to try to see if I could really play the lead guitar in front of an audience. Without admitting it, I knew this was the safest place for me to try and, if it happened, to fail. After all, we were all in a psychiatric hospital. Andy still refused to participate unless he could fart. Tony said: "Andy, Hamlet needs a ghost, so if you cover yourself in a sheet, you can be part of the revue without being part of it." I wasn't sure if

Tony really had a diplomatic side to him or if he intended to suffocate Andy in the sheet, but I was beginning to realize that I didn't need to try to control everything. I also knew it was very dangerous for Tony to try to include Andy in his act, but my therapy had educated me enough to let him feel his own pain.

We refined, argued, and stumbled towards as much a cohesive act as addicts could. We never rehearsed together. Too many egos, too many conflicts. It wasn't until Skit Night itself that we were able to determine the line-up. All of the patients and all of the staff packed the room. The domes went in random order. We wound up being last and the women were first.

Before they went on Pam said: "We're going to suck. We only came up with the final idea last night. We're all going to be members of the staff while pretending that Karen is a patient," which is what they did. The hostility was remarkable. They really got into tearing Karen apart "for the purpose of healing her." I was sure the staff would actually staff that performance the next morning.

There were many funny moments and starry eyed laughing. The dentist who wanted to have a band sing "Louie Louie" stood in front of the crowd and sang it solo and a capella. The only lyrics he could remember consisted of the title. He just sort of moaned the rest. He went on and on until someone started clapping. Then the rest of us cheered and clapped which got him to stop.

One of the other male domes dressed up in women's underwear and sang Monty Python's "Lumberjack song." The rest of the domes struggled through parodies of therapy groups and imitations of the staff. Then it was our turn.

Brand stood up in front of the crowd in his church clothes. He introduced himself as "Dick Clark" and said: "We have the revue of revues! Let me introduce to you, The Professor!"

The Professor had been hiding in the bathroom and came out only after Brand went to get him. Then the Professor walked in front of the crowd. He wore a sheet, dyed orange, toga style. He had orange makeup on and had dyed his hair green. He waited for the hoots to die down and said: "I was told when I was young that carrots were good for me but that I must be aware of my family's carrot addiction gene. I ignored my family's warning. I could not resist my own nature."

He dramatically paused after each sentence, as though he were tendering his confession. "I went to the Culinary Institute to learn more about the true love of my life. I got my PhD in carrotology. I loved eating them raw or cooked, whether boiled, steamed, baked, sautéed. Once in the south, I learned to deep fry them. They are always delicious." The audience loved it.

"In college, I noticed that the tips of my ears looked orange in the sunlight. I told myself it was only a tan. The ends of my hair started turning green, so contrary to the style of the day I kept my hair cut short and told my contemporaries that I was simply a non-conformist. In graduate school, my skin became orange, fibrous green hair grew on my legs and arms, so I always wore long pants and long sleeved shirts. I only went swimming at night. I only made love in the dark. When my first wife saw me naked, she collapsed and filed for divorce the next day."

With each line, he got a more tortured and tragic look on his face. " After she first saw me naked, my second wife developed such a laughing disorder that she had to be hospitalized. I learned to daily shave my skin from my toes to my eyebrows and wore body make-up, legal only in Turkey. Each of these efforts to appear normal was nothing to me. There was no burden too great to bear to sustain my love for carrots. Now you see me as I truly am. I stand in front of you naked and proud! Soon, I will myself become edible. I cannot wait for the day when I finally am able to eat myself!"

I wished that he had done his bit ahead of the rest of us because his act was so good, it seemed impossible to follow. Next was Michael, who had also refused to give us a preview.

Brand introduced him, saying, "Here's Michael and he's going to do something he calls "Bird Calls."

Michael stood in front of the audience with only a flashlight. "Will you please turn off all the lights," he said, which was done. He turned on the flashlight and aimed it at the ceiling. Flickering it back and forth he said: "Bird calls" and started whistling. He said: "Cardinal" and pointed the flashlight at a woman in the audience who wore a red blouse. He started whistling again. He said: "Chicken" and pointed the light at a member of the staff we all thought was cowardly. He whistled some more and kept flashing the light around the room. He aimed the light at two women patients who were rumored to be involved with each other: "Love birds." He whistled some more and then, pointing the light at Pam, said: "Mockingbird." He whistled again, pointing the light over the faces of many in the audience. Finally, he lit up Karen's face and said: "Big Bird." She laughed so hard she had tears in her eyes. He hooted a few times, shined the flashlight on himself, bowed and sat down.

It was Billy's turn to sing. The lights were turned back on. I turned on my amp and plugged my guitar in. Southern Boy stood next to Billy and started playing the chords to "All Along the Watchtower." Billy sang:

> "There must be some way out of here,"
> said the dentist to the shrink.
> "I can't get no drugs,
> I need some relief.
> Businessmen they drink my wine,
> Nurses drink my beer.
> No matter what I do,
> I can't get my urine clear."
> "No reason to get excited,"
> the surgeon kindly spoke,
> "My lawyer is coming
> with drugs inside his chest.
> All we need is a scalpel
> he's really got the best."

Then it was time for my lead. This was a big deal to me. I had only played in public once and because I wasn't perfect, I left the stage. I saw that Cliff was looking right at me, so I looked at my fingers and just played. I made one mistake, but for once it didn't seem to matter. While I was playing, Cliff stood up, cheered and hollered, and so did the rest of the audience. Billy went back to singing and the Southern Boy grinned. For me, this was more than a true event. It was an entry into life.

The final bit was Tony's "Hamlet." He stood in front of the audience with arrogance and servitude, like an actor who really believed he was truly gifted but had been taught that it was poor taste to acknowledge that belief. As the audience quieted down, Tony placed a skull and a cardboard tube on the floor. He loudly said: "These are my things." He took a large audible breath and said: "To drug, or not to drug, that is the question." That was his best line. He wore Shakespeare down with rigorous sincerity, only matched by the way Andy daily wore Tony down.

As Tony said: "When we have shuffled off this mortal coil," a large person covered in a white sheet walked up behind Tony and said: "Tony?" Tony?" Tony looked startled but continued with his lines. "....Must give us pause," he said and then paused. At that moment, at that very precise moment, at that moment which was so precise and so exact only NASA or God Himself could have planned and executed it, the ghost farted. Tony turned red but gave no other indication that he had heard the noise. He bent over to pick up the skull and as he did, the sheet covered figure bent with him in unison and farted again. Tony did not move but the audience did. At first, there was just a titter of giggles then the sheeted person grabbed the cardboard tube, rose and ran around Tony saying his name over and over in semi-ghostly tones through the tube: "Tony! Tony!" The ghost stretched out each syllable as though it were Silly Putty. It was so obvious. And, of course, it was so Andy. The audience loved it just like a Jerry Springer audience loves the fight between the lesbian lovers, the drag queens and their straight boyfriends, and the poor souls who have nothing left to show and share but anger and shame. Andy had a gift for appealing to these qualities.

Tony started spitting out the rest of his lines, but they were lost in the laughter. Each time he said a line, Andy farted. Finally, Tony shouted out his last rewritten lines: "With this regard, the drugs turn awry, and lose the name of their brand—but Take you now!" He glared at Andy with slings and arrows. Andy, still covered in his sheet, but audibly laughing with the audience, stood still. He raised his arms and the audience quieted down and as they did, he didn't fart, instead he let out a belch that must have been stored in a reservoir so deep that it took an inhuman ability to access it. The belch didn't burp, it roared. And as it did, so did the audience. Tony turned and left the room. Andy collapsed on the floor with the sheet covering him. The audience was still laughing and then Andy stood up saying "Tony! Tony!" in his ghost-like tones. Raising and lowering his sheet covered arms, he too left the room.

Brand then stood up, straightened his church tie, smoothed out his church vest and said: "That concludes the entertainment portion of our program." Billy looked at me and said: "I wonder if the staff pay Andy to torture Tony so that he'll stay here longer."

Forgiveness – It's The Law!

Family week was coming up. This was a five-day period when the family members of the patients who would come, came to the treatment center where special family groups were held to discuss the patient and "families of origin issues." It was a good idea because patients often had warped, twisted or simply wrong memories and perceptions of their family and their family history. Lots of times, too, the patient's memories were right. There was lots of yelling and screaming in the family groups. In good groups, which were groups which accomplished something, there were lots of tears.

Unknown to me, Cliff and Sally, my "family" counselor, had been making arrangements with my sister Bev to have my other sister, both of my brothers and my mother come to family week. I got very angry that they had been arranging this. My family counselor told me that my family would only be allowed to come if I approved it. I said: "My brothers and sisters can come, but not my mother."

Every counselor I had started putting pressure on me to include my mother. I came up with every graceful excuse I could: "She's too old and too ill." "She never knew my dad sexually abused me." "This will be too hard for her." Every excuse was met with reasonable discussion, which drove me nuts. I didn't want reasonable discussion. I just wanted to yell: "No!" Finally, my sister Bev told me that her daughter said: "Grandmother has been through the Depression, World War II, Korea, Vietnam and Grandpa. She's tough."

As family week approached, the discussion in all the groups

centered around how to deal with our individual families. We spent a lot of time identifying issues to discuss, identifying our feelings and how to use our language. We used language as an art form. We made jokes to deflect criticism. We'd insist upon definitions of common words hoping that the discussion would get caught up in a debate because once the other person agreed to define words, we had won because the discussion went from listening to debate. And we never lost debates because the other person had agreed that word definition came first which meant we got to define everything. The staff called this behavior "character defects" or, more charitably, "obstacles to recovery." I called it survival.

It took me a long time to realize it, but I was afraid of being hurt by my mother. My niece was right: she was tough. She had always been tough, so tough, that instead of love, I felt judgment and rejection. I saw others who had appeared to have been nursed by the myth of mother love and felt jealous, alone, empty and isolated. I lived in a bubble of maternal rejection. No one could be funnier, more charming, or more caring than me. No one could also be more alone. Try to get close to me and I'd keep you laughing. If you didn't laugh, or if I began to like you too much, I'd simply cut you off. No one else would ever reject me. I would charm them and then drop them. It served them right for liking me in the first place.

I had learned the art of cut-offs from two masters. At one of my birthday dinners when I was in my twenties, my father refused to eat with us or even talk with any of us.

At the time of the cutting of the cake, my mother asked him: "Charlie, aren't you going to at least have cake with us?"

He said: "No, who'd want to eat any of that dry, crumbling cake you make?" with a tone of voice that was both fire and ice.

I looked at him and said: "Dad, all these years I thought we learned that tone of voice from mom, and now I discover we learned it from you."

He looked at me with eyes that had gone black and calmly said: "I studied under your mother," as he walked into his bedroom.

At another birthday dinner, she was putting pressure on me to "find a nice girl and get married." These conversations always made me nervous, because I didn't want a nice girl. I wanted a jock, a swimmer, sailor, tennis player, wrestler or baseball star. It didn't matter.

My dad overheard her and said: "Shut up Bernice! Do you want him to be as miserable as we are?"

One was dead and one was living, but both had been dead to me a long time.

The week before family week, Cliff took me aside and said: "Ron, if you don't have your mother here, you may never recover. You need to tell her how you feel."

I started my excuses again, which he interrupted. He asked: "I understand one of your brothers has just been diagnosed with cancer?"

I said: "Yes, my brother Rick, the day before yesterday. I'm not sure which cancer he has, but it's in stage four."

Cliff had been around. He said: "That's the final stage." I started crying.

Cliff said: "What are you thinking?"

I mumbled: "I'm just beginning to realize how much he must love me to still be coming. He's putting off his chemotherapy for a week to do this."

Cliff said: "This may be the only time you all can be together to do this."

Then he put in the trick that he must have known would work by saying: "And this can be healing for all of them too, not just you."

Ah, yes, he already knew me. Appeal to my sense of sacrifice, martyrdom and rescuing. Where was that cape? Right next to the light-saber. Still crying, but trying to look noble, I said: "okay. She can come."

I doubt that I really had anything to do with the decision of her coming, that was being made by others, but it was important for me to think that I had some lingering influence in my own life. He smiled and hugged me. I used to recoil at such touches, but for some reason I trusted him. I had so treasured my wounds, creating a reality in which they could not be nursed. But, with his touch and his words, I heard the faint bell ringing of a chime of freedom.

For the first day of family week, we were only allowed to see our various family members in the corridor. They had their own program of lectures and groups for a day and a half. We couldn't talk to them about anything substantive until the second day. We couldn't even have dinner with them.

I found my sisters in the hall, hugged them and said: "Promise me you won't mention about dad sexually abusing me." Bonnie, my oldest sister, asked: "Why not?" I knew she was right. She had been horribly abused by him and had no reason or desire to protect him. Now that he was dead, only perceptions, memories and continued behaviors could hurt her.

I started to argue with her, but Bev interrupted and said: "None of us will do anything to hurt you." I wanted to discuss this more, but they were called away.

I tried to talk about all this with Andy, but he simply smiled and said: "My family is never coming. I will never allow it."

Pam was more open. Her husband was there. She too was nervous, but she said: "Hey, we've been fucked up too long! Trust Bev. No one's here to hurt you."

Intellectually, I knew that, but I was still so afraid. I was also so angry. How could my mother have let my dad hurt us all like he did? Why didn't she do anything? Pam said: "Ron, you know it was different back then. She probably didn't see any options."

I said: "Pam, she is a very smart woman. She could have seen them. She just loved him and the abuse more than she loved us."

Pam said: "Yeah, just like you're a very smart man and you love your own abuse and abusing others. C'mon, Ron, you've got to look at yourself too. What's your part in this?"

I didn't say anything. I hated looking at my part in things. She grabbed my arm, smiled and said: "Let's go to lunch."

We walked in silence down the path to the hospital cafeteria. That smell of nutmeg was there, somewhere in the woods. I said: "Pam, stop. Do you smell that?"

She said: "No. Smell what?"

I said: "Some Christmas smell of nutmeg coming from those pines."

She stood still, closed her eyes and breathed deeply. "No. I don't."

I said: "It's nearly overpowering to me. And it's only in this little area."

She laughed a little and said: "Well, you could be psychotic, smelling things that aren't there."

She must have seen the look of panic on my face. She knew I gave anyone with a medical background great credence in these kinds of diagnoses.

"Ron, I'm just kidding. Don't be so sensitive. Just because I can't smell it doesn't mean it's not there."

We kept walking to the cafeteria. There was a long line once we got there. During family week, the meals improved dramatically, which probably explained the line. As we waited, Father Liam came running up and asked if he could cut in line with us.

I said: "Like if we said 'no,' it would make a difference?"

He laughed and said: "No, Ron, it wouldn't make a difference."

Pam and I were silent and Liam looked at both of us and said: "How's it going. Seen any of your families yet?"

Pam said that she had seen her husband for a special one-on-one with their family counselor that morning and that it was rough, but that it went all right. She said she had started listening to him.

Then he looked at me. "What about you, Ron?"

I said: "I saw my sisters in the hallway. That's it."

He asked: "You haven't seen your mother yet?"

I answered: "No. I think she's with my brothers."

He smiled and said: "Good, good."

I said: "What's so good about it. Liam, I really am very angry at her. Should I tell her that?"

He said: "You can if you want, but you should really look at what the anger is covering up."

"That's easy," I said, "lack of love, no protection from abuse..."
I wanted to go on, but he interrupted me and said: "Oh, Ron, your hate
will kill you. It almost already has. It's toughened your heart into black
tar like a smoker's lung."

"Oh, is that the Black Irish diagnosis? Well, what am I supposed
to feel?" I asked.

"You're supposed to feel your feelings. But you also need to
learn to forgive."

"Forgive? In today's world, my dad would be in prison for what
he did."

"Yes," he said, "I suppose he would. And in some very real
ways, you would be too, for what you've done. So would I. So would
Pam. Not that prison would do anyone any good: help the world or
solve any problems. It would only make the anger of all of you to
become bigger and more harmful than the prison itself. Remember, we
are all saints and sinners."

"Liam," I said, "None of the Catholic crap, please."

He said nothing, but just smiled. I turned my back on him. I
was facing jail, and it scared the shit out of me. Even though no one else
thought I would go to jail, I knew I would. I had to. I had been waiting
my whole life to go to jail. I deserved it.

I turned my back on him. The line was very slow. He and Pam
started talking about something.

I turned around and said: "okay, Liam, just how am I supposed
to forgive her?"

He looked up at me and said: "Start with some small measure of compassion. I know you've got it in you. The other patients are always coming to you to talk about their sins. Whether you know it or not, you're some kind of fucked-up wanna-be-Jesuit, which is its own problem. But you've got compassion."

"Compassion?" I was shocked. Compassion for the woman who let all of us be victimized in our individual ways?

"Liam," I said, "My dad used my oldest sister's and brother's heads to make holes in the ceilings. He would pick them up and bounce their heads into the ceiling. He followed them around the house one time breaking all the dishes over their heads while they were running to get away from him. He'd break furniture on them. He smashed my mother's face into the four corners of the kitchen table once when she danced with his boss at an office party."

Liam looked at me very seriously. He said: "I'm not saying this to diminish your pain, which is very real, but, as horrible as all that was and is, neither you nor they are alone. Look around you. This place is full of abused children who learned abuse very well. Let me ask you if you haven't become your father."

I got so mad I turned crimson. I started to turn away again. "Don't turn away, Ron, this may be your last chance for freedom."

I turned back to him with tears of rage in my eyes. "You don't understand."

He said: "Oh, Ron, I do. I'm here too, remember. I'm an alcoholic too. And I never got into recovery until after both my parents were dead. In some ways, you're lucky."

"Lucky?" I asked, getting close to debate.

Liam laughed again and said: "Oh, Ron, I'm not going to play the debate game with you. Besides the fact that you're so good at it, it's meaningless. Just take the words as I say them and for their common meaning. You're lucky just to be here and not in jail, on the street or dead. You're very good at feeling sorry for yourself. You do it with wonderful nuance, but it's still very harmful and self-destructive. You are a misplaced gentle soul, trapped by your victimization, hate, anger and you've become a victimizer. I know how you are aching. Quit stringing yourself out with beautiful words and find your feelings."

This got me smiling. "Ah, the Jungian/Star Wars connection, eh?"

He said: "And quit with the Star Wars crap."

I turned away again. I was so miserable. I hated my life. I had wanted to die. When the alcohol, pills and sex hadn't killed me fast enough, I had very carefully planned a wonderful and dramatic suicide. But I also loved laughing with Pam and Andy, sharing stories and pain. I loved the other patients talking with me. I loved the attention from staff. I especially loved the gentle touches and hugs of Cliff. More importantly, I loved how he talked with me, his direction and his compassion.

The line slowly moved. Just before we got to the place where we picked up our trays and silverware, I asked Liam: "Okay, and how do I use this famous compassion of yours?"

"Just think," he answered, "how she felt seeing her babies hurt, how she felt alone and helpless, how deep her pain was and how little she thought of herself. In her era, she probably thought she was being punished for some unknown sin and that this was her punishment."

He continued: "I've seen you do this with other patients. And when you think of her, realize that you and your brothers and sisters were part of her pain, her punishment and pleasure. I'm not saying any of this is rational. It was probably her fucked-up self image, delivered to her as a Trojan horse gift from her parents, just as yours was given to you by your parents. Try to treat her as you would these other patients or a sick best friend."

Of course, I was crying again. It seemed as though the line and time itself had stopped. I felt as though I had been struck by lightning. I looked at him again. He said: "You are a searching soul. You are a lonesome hearted lover, misplaced, but you can be found again. But only you can be the seeker."

I smiled again and said: "Is it just the Irish accent, or are you really making sense?"

He laughed and said: "Oh, probably a little of both, but the accent helps a lot in America. In England, though, they'd lock me up." He laughed that Irish cackle laugh again and said: "Compassion will lead to forgiveness. Imagine how horrible your parents' backgrounds must have been: All those gifts and all that pain."

I said nothing for a moment. The line started shuffling forward again. I said: "okay," and moved forward.

How did he know this? I had always felt like a misplaced soldier of love. It was easy for me to talk to others. Cliff himself had said: "Ron, you are a master of deeply superficial relationships." I was so scared, though, of a real relationship. Afraid, I knew, of what others took in so easily.

Pam, Liam and I sat down together. They started in with patient gossip, which we weren't supposed to do but which we all did gleefully.

Normally, I was an expert at this, but Cliff had said to me: "Do you realize that, for you, gossip is a drug? When you gossip, you're using. And you can't get into recovery if you're using."

After lunch, we went back up the hill. There was a note on the corkboard message center for me from Cliff: "You have permission to have dinner with your family. You are to take Andy and Kevin with you. Meet your family at their hotel at 6:00 p.m. All of you have permission to skip your in-house AA meeting tonight. But you still have to make a later one."

At house group that afternoon, Kathy asked the three of us if we have received our notes. Andy said: "Hell yes, I want Ron to have to pay for a good meal for me."

She asked Kevin if he'd go. He said: "Sure."

Kathy then said: "okay. No talking about Fabian family issues. You can discuss what we do here, how it works, the rules and what it's like to live here. But, no family issues until family groups start tomorrow."

We went from house group to the Dome where we told the Senior Addict what was going on. He said: "I know. See you guys later."

Brand was, typically, upset. "I don't know why the three of you get special treatment. It's not fair. This is just proof of you sucking up to Cliff."

I said: "Brand, be good and we'll bring you back a doggie bag."

Andy said: "But you only get it if you clean the shit out of your doghouse."

I was very nervous on the drive over. Kevin was very

supportive. "This won't be that bad. Your family has got to have some positive stuff going on."

He was right. They were all very charming, even kind. Just not to me, I thought. Just not to me.

We met them in the lobby. They had apparently received some marching orders too, because the discussion was lively but not deep. Kevin and Andy though, were very generous and open about their own problems. They started telling other patient stories which seemed to put everyone else at ease, especially after they heard the story about the doctor whose kid died in the house fire when he was out buying his drugs. My problems certainly looked small in comparison.

We had to leave to make an AA meeting across town. This was a speaker meeting, where an addict or alcoholic talked about their background, their struggles and their recovery. Tonight the speaker was a black woman.

"Hey," she said, "my name is Kimberly and I'm an alcoholic. And, an addict."

Those in the room yelled back: "Welcome Kimberly."

She started talking about her home life, her abuse, her drug use. I really didn't listen much. I was thinking more about me and my family. Kevin must have seen that I was distracted because he elbowed me in the ribs.

"Listen up, Ron," he said.

Kimberly said: "Even after I got into recovery, I still wouldn't talk with my mother. I still held onto the resentment of why she didn't protect me. My dad had abused me, my grandfather had sex with me, and she ignored me."

This did get my attention.

She went on: "After I was in recovery for about three years, I had a birthday party. You know, the real kind, cake, ice cream and all that. There were lots of people there. The only person not there was my mother. And then I started thinking: "I have an abundance of love. If I have this much love, why can't I share it with the person who needs it the most. My mother was the most hung-out person I had ever met. Probably the most hung-out in the whole universe. So, after the party, I went to her house. I'm not sure if she was glad to see me, but because of that visit she's glad to see me now and I'm glad to see her."

I waited. What was this magic? She said: "In recovery we learn there's no magic. When we were using, we were using the sick magic of drugs and alcohol. Magic is instant, just like the effects of sex and drugs. But in recovery we learn that miracles happen. And the miracles happen not because we plan them, but because we let them."

"Let a miracle happen?" What the fuck did that mean?

Kimberly said: "So I sat down with my mama and said: 'Mama, I've hurt you and you've hurt me. I want to get beyond that. I have an abundance of love, and I want to share it.' And she must have been waiting for that miracle because she started to cry, and I cried, and we hugged. I'm not saying we're the best of friends, but we live in our love now and not our misery."

I was stunned. She said something else, which I don't remember and then the meeting ended. Kevin and Andy were ready to go, but I said: "Wait, I've got to talk to her."

She was surrounded by a few people, talking with them. I waited for my turn. She looked at me and said: "Oh, here's an aching one." I didn't know my feelings were so obvious.

I walked up to her, crying as she hugged me. I sobbed: "How did you do it? How did you do it?"

She said: "Honey, I can tell you're full of love. You just have to share it and give it away. You'll get way more. I bet you've got way more than you need yourself. You're just busting with love."

I kept hugging her and sobbing. "How did you do it?"

She held me at arm's length looking me directly in the face. "Honey," I loved being called 'honey.' I thought I could never get too much of that. She said, "I just gave away what I already had. Barn swallows have love. Dogs and cats have love. Even if you don't believe in God, you got to see the love everywhere. I can feel it in you. I can see your face. Give away your love and get rid of your pain and misery. That's the miracle. The more you give the more you get."

I ran my sleeve under my nose. "Oh, no," I said, "More Beatles." She laughed and said, "Honey, they didn't invent that. They just sang about it. You can live it. Now, who are you mad at?"

I said: "My mother, same as you."

She said: "Honey, you go hug her and tell her you love her."

"Oh," I said, still crying, "Will the gates of heaven open then?"

"My," she said, "You really do hurt don't you?" I nodded my head.

"Don't expect heaven to open. It's already open. The miracle is realizing that. There are lots of gentle souls misplaced inside of jails, whether the jails have bars or not. You don't have to live in them. You can live in heaven here."

She didn't rush me. She just kept looking at me with incredible kindness and soft, deep eyes.

I glanced at Kevin and Andy. She said: "Are those your friends?" I nodded.

She said: "Well, they'll wait. You don't have to hurry off. I'll hug you as long as you want."

"That would be forever," I said. She laughed and then she lifted her hand and brushed my bangs across my forehead.

"Honey, I can see love all over you. Go share it. Forgive others and you get forgiven. That's the law."

I laughed. She laughed. I said: "That's the best law I ever heard."

I hugged her tight once more and said: "Thanks."

She said: "Remember when you are hugging your mama that she'll be waiting, and she'll be hugging back."

The drive back was mostly quiet. I reached to put in a CD and Andy said: "No magical mystery tour crap."

I said: "Nope" but put George Harrison on.

When we got back, I went straight to my room. Eddy asked: "How'd it go man?"

I related the whole day to him. He laughed. I said: "Why are you laughing?"

He said: "It was all set up. The staff meet for two hours every morning. During family week, they fully discuss each patient whose family is here. Then they do the set-ups they think are necessary to get things going."

I was amazed. "I don't believe you," I said.

"Ron," he said, "You know how many treatment centers I've

been in. I used to work with Cliff at another treatment center."

I started getting angry. "So, all of this is false? Everything Liam and Cliff said to me?"

"No," he said, "Not false, just calculated. Hey, man, it's just good treatment. It means they are paying attention to you. And, believe me, with all this attention they must think you're ready to change and accept recovery or they'd be doing other things. They'd be treating you like they treat Brand. Don't forget that right now this is your reality. And it's all about very real stuff."

I struggled to say: "I thought maybe this was because they sort of loved me."

Eddy said: "They do, man. You are very lovable. It's one reason Brand hates you so much. He doesn't understand that love, acceptance and forgiveness are the keys. Look at him as you would your dad. Step back, or fly up, or do whatever is necessary to distance yourself and look at all this as it is."

I got into bed, saying nothing. After he got into his bed, I asked: "Eddy, does this mean that you being my roommate is no accident?"

He was silent for a minute. I couldn't see him, but I knew he was stroking his beard by his left chin.

He said: "I wonder about that too, and no, I don't think it's an accident. You see I have no faith. None whatsoever. And you are abundant in faith, whether you know it or not. Everything you say has faith in it, even when you are putting 'The Christians' down. You get pissed at their protestations of faith while you keep yours so secret. I think you get upset with them because you have such a finely honed sense of hypocrisy, and that is why you get upset with yourself so much.

But you nearly get consumed by it too."

I said: "What do you mean by that?"

He said: "You are so hard on yourself."

He was quiet for a minute and then said: "Ron, I think you'd forgive the guy that killed John Lennon before you would forgive yourself for leaving an ice cream stick on the sidewalk."

"Eddy," I said, "I've had too many opinions about myself today to take in anything else. I do have some kind of blind faith in something, I don't know what. And I would forgive the guy who killed John. It's almost as though his crime is his own punishment. But I would like to have the other three reunite in a huge concert and release the guy in the crowd to see if Beatle fans really bought John's 'all you need is love' message."

By the way Eddy laughed, I could tell he was still stroking his beard. "Okay, man, go to sleep. But if you can think of a way to give me some of that faith, do it."

I feel asleep thinking about faith and worrying about tomorrow.

I drove to campus the next day with Kevin and Andy. They were both giving me so much advice I said: "Shut the fuck up." They wouldn't let go, so I wound up focusing on them and their crap, but I put George Harrison music on the car's compact disc player.

After morning spiritual and a first-step delivery, I went to my first family group session. My family was already there with Sally, the family counselor. They were all seated, so I sat in the only chair left, between Sally and Rick and across from my mother. Another set-up, I thought.

Sally said: "Well, now that we're all here, who'd like to start?"

No one said anything. Then Rick said: "Well, life is too short to waste any time, so let's talk about how dad sexually abused Ron."

I was shocked and mad. I said: "Bev gave me her promise we wouldn't discuss this."

Rick smiled his little boy grin and said: "That was her promise, not mine."

I said: "That's why I didn't get to see you alone yesterday."

He smiled again and said: "Maybe. But I've got seniority in here due to the shortness of time. So let's get serious."

We got serious. My mother said: "What? He did what?"

So like the lawyer I was, I calmly told her what had happened, when it had happened, and how it made me feel.

She started to deny that it could ever have happened. "I would have known!"

Bonnie said: "Mom, there's a lot that happened that you didn't know."

Bev said: "Or wouldn't know."

Bob just sat there, white, with a very drawn and tight face. I looked at him and started to cry. He had been so beat-up, so wounded. This must be incredibly difficult for him, to relive the past he had tried so hard to bury, to deny and ignore. It must have been like opening a long-buried coffin with the horror of the smells of death and decrepit flesh assaulting his unprotected senses. This was a major sacrifice for him. To come all this way to relive his horrible past was more than fraternal duty, it was brotherly love. And I was upset with myself for having been nervous. Talk about being spoiled. I tried to distance myself, as Eddy had suggested, and I flew up in a helicopter but not, this time, out of my body. This time I stayed in my body and used this gift, if that is what it was, to see these people for what they were: all wounded souls living a life that mostly just happened to them.

My mother started to talk about how bad things happened sometimes. Sally said, in a voice of command, "Bernice, remember what we talked about. We are here not to discuss facts or to debate. We are here to deal with Ron's feelings." I had never heard anyone use a voice like that with my mother. Besides being commanding, it was reassuring. How did she do that, I wondered?

Sally looked at me and said: "How are you feeling?"

I didn't know what to say. I looked at my mother and said: "I feel hurt. I feel rejected. I feel as though I have never been loved. I feel that no one ever loved me until Craig came into my life." We all started to cry then. He had been so important to all of us. "Since his death, I have been crazy. And I'm afraid I'm becoming Dad."

They must have received some marching orders from Sally, because no one spoke. My mother finally said: "You are my baby. And I love you."

We all sat in silence. Was this, too, orchestrated by staff? Had Sally, Liam, Cliff and Kathy planned it all? I remembered what Eddy said last night about faith and how he thought I had so much.

I consciously let the faith in a bit and said to myself: "Okay. This couldn't have been that orchestrated. As full of cynicism as you are, these are your brothers and sisters. And they must have some of that love and faith that you do. They are here. Think about Rick. He put off his chemotherapy to be here. Look at Bob. He is still white." Even though he was looking at his feet, I could see the tears in his eyes.

Bonnie said: "Ron, we all love you. We always have. We just didn't know how to tell you. We have put up such walls around ourselves, and none better than you."

Bob said: "You were always like an alien to the rest of us."

Bev said: "Not me." She was right. Not her.

I looked at Bob and said: "Bob, that's how I felt, too."

Bonnie said: "Not an alien. Just a little weird."

I started to say something but Sally interrupted and said: "Let's hear from Rick."

Rick looked at me with tears in his eyes too. "I never called you weird. I just never knew how to talk with you." He got very angry. "I knew something must have happened because you spent your teenage years sleeping, reading and hiding." He tightened his fists and said: "Goddamn dad! And I told you to leave that goddamned small town! This would never have happened if you had moved to Ann Arbor. You could have found someone. You would have found someone."

Our mother was still quiet. She repeated: "I never knew. I never knew."

I was so torn. Here was my time to crap all over her if I wanted. Or I could be the wonderful hero son and pretend I hadn't been hurt. I really didn't know what to do. So, I said nothing but started to cry too.

None of us said anything for a long time. Time didn't seem frozen, it seemed endless. I was remembering every little slight that had ever happened to me. I also remembered the acts of kindness, love and support. This was so strange I didn't know how to react. Sally said: "Ron, how are you feeling?"

I said: "I don't know." She stood and said: "Good. Let's just hug."

Bonnie and Bev stood with their arms out. Rick looked at me and said: "Oprah Time!" I laughed.

Bob just sat there, next to our mom. He was crying so hard there was snot coming out of his nose. I was still a little pissed, but I was so used to hugging here, and I knew how good it felt. There would be no sexual touches here. Sally was here. Cliff was down the hall. My next group was with him. If it wasn't safe here, it wasn't safe anywhere.

I stood up and said: "C'mon Bob, it really doesn't hurt. It actually sort of helps."

He and my mother stood together. We all put our arms around each other and did nothing but cry. No one said anything. Rick was crying the hardest. After a while, I pulled back and asked him what he was crying about.

He said: "Me, you, my kids and us as kids."

Bob said: "I just don't remember so much."

Beverly went around us all, initiating individual hugs. After hugging Bev, Bonnie, Bob and Rick, I went to my mother and hugged her. She looked up at me and said: "I always loved you. How could you not know that?'

Sally looked at me. I said: "I just didn't. That's all."

Sally said: "okay. That's it for right now. Ron has a group he has to go to."

I said: "Oh, I can be late."

She said: "No, you can't. We'll all catch up later."

I went to my mother, hugged her and said: "I love you." She was so tiny in my arms, powerful and weak at the same time. She hugged back and, crying, said: "I love you too."

So I left the room with all of them crying and went into Cliff's group.

When I walked in, Cliff said: "How'd it go?"

I said: "I'm not sure."

He said: "That's good. If you were sure, then you wouldn't have really been there."

I started to ask him what he meant, but he went on and said: "You know what I noticed about your family?"

I said: "No, what?"

He said: "They all have very kind eyes. Think about that."

I started to think about it and then the fire alarm went off. He got up, opened the door and stood next to it. None of us moved and we couldn't talk because the alarm was so loud. Cliff looked at us all with a look of wonder and disgust.

He shouted: "How loud does an alarm have to be before you hear it? Get the hell out of here!" I started giggling because he seemed so serious. He glared at me as I giggled.

I said: "Yes, teacher" and went out the door.

There was no smoke in the hallway, but the light was weird. The normal, fluorescent ceiling lights had gone out. Flickering bright, blue-white strobe lights had come on. The light in the hallway alternated between gray darkness and intense brightness. Someone yelled: "Embrace the light!" Someone else yelled: "No! Stay away from the light! It's not your time!" I just kept giggling.

The hallway became crowded and the parade of patients walked quickly down the corridor. As I passed the doors to other treatment rooms, other therapists and patients opened the doors to their rooms and looked at those of us who were in the hall.

One therapist made eye contact with me and shouted: "What's going on?" I shouted back: "You're asking me? You're the therapist! If you don't know, I want my money back!"

Pam had been standing behind the therapist, walked around her and shouted: "That's a Freudian for you. Always looking for something more than the obvious. Sometimes a fire alarm is just a fire alarm."

She put her arm around me, leaned in close and said: "This reminds me of an Airplane concert in 1968 in San Francisco. Everyone was too doped to move."

The hall became crowed with patients and staff who were now shouting at all of us to move. Pam and I got separated. I became part of a tight crowd of patients I didn't know. We walked very close to each other. We turned the final corner of the hall and went out onto the patio.

Karen was standing there, holding one of the doors open, shouting: "Move out onto the grass! Move out onto the grass!"

A patient yelled back: "Now you're telling us to break rules!"

Karen yelled back: "Shut the fuck up and move your ass!"

When I got to the grass, I stopped, turned around and looked at the building. There was no smoke coming from it. The alarm kept ringing and the strobes kept flashing. I looked at the people around me. I knew none of them. Standing right next to me was a very good looking short guy who appeared to be in his mid-thirties.

He turned, looked at me with a very goofy look on his face and said: "Hi. I'm Terry. Who are you?"

His accent identified him as being from the very Deep South.

His look identified him as being very fucked up and maybe not too bright. He kept smiling showing absolutely perfect teeth.

I smiled back, held out my hand and said: "I'm Ron."

He looked down at my hand, back up at me, and said: "Oh, I guess I'm supposed to shake your hand."

He grabbed it, shook it, and looked at me with his perfect teeth smile. I was in love.

I said: "Hi Terry. Been here long?"

He looked at me as though I had asked him to tell me where and when Napoleon was born or Obi-Wan-Kenobi's birth name.

After a long moment he smiled again and said: "Two days. Let me see. Yep, today is the second day."

"You mean on campus?" I said.

He looked at me again as though I had asked the most obscure question.

After a very long moment, he said: "I think I spent the night in a hospital. I came to this building yesterday afternoon. So I think that's two days."

I thought it would be better if I asked a very simple question: "What do you do for a living?"

He smiled again. Jeez! That smile was perfect. I felt like I could spend my whole life staring at that smile. He answered much more quickly this time.

"I'm a dentist." I loved how, when he spoke, each syllable had long, lazy sounds. "Eye-uh ah-m uhhhhh dehn-ni-tist."

I smiled with my non-perfect teeth and said: "I should have guessed."

He looked at me with surprise. I said: "Your teeth are perfect."

He acted as though he were waking up a little. "Oh, yeah, they were done in dental school." He added: "For free. Because I was a student."

I asked: "Well, if you're a dentist, your drug of choice was probably nitrous oxide, right?"

Did that smile ever leave his face? He took less time to answer and said: "No. Though that was nice. I liked beer."

"Beer?" I asked. "Beer? That was enough to get you in here?" Beer didn't make sense. He looked like a soccer player. He had absolutely no gut.

He kept smiling. "Oh, and I used to take a lot of Hydrocodone."

He stopped with that. Then he said: "I'd get a six pack on the way home every night. I'd start drinking while driving home and I'd pop a few pills with the beer." He was waking up more now, but he still looked very goofy.

He kept talking: "I'd walk by my wife and my daughter, go to my rec room, turn on the TV, and drink the beer and take more pills until I passed out."

I was silent for a moment. I wanted to make him feel okay. "I used to drink vodka martinis every night and mix them with Codeine and Vicodin." He smiled that goofy smile again. I was in love. And I knew that an instant feeling like that was dangerous. In the old days, I'd have us both drunk and in bed by sundown. Again, for the second time that day, I remembered what Eddy said: "Get some distance, man."

This guy triggered something in me. It wasn't just because he was good looking or goofy. As I looked at him, he kept talking about his drugs and how his daughter died. He said something about her being duct-taped to various chairs and her hair being duct-taped.

I looked at him and said: "Is that how she died?"

He looked back at me as though I were the goofy one and said: "No. She died in the car accident." I must have had an odd look on my face. He said: "It had nothing to do with my wife. My daughter was with a friend and a car hit them both."

He then started talking about the car accident. So many accidents, I thought. It's an accident that I'm standing here, next to him, which I wouldn't be doing without the fire alarm. This meeting, certainly, could not have been arranged and orchestrated. If it had, it hadn't been by the staff. If this man was a present. He wasn't here to satisfy my sex life or fantasies. If Liam or Cliff or whomever had arranged all this, I wanted some of whatever they had.

I kept thinking: "How could I like him so instantly and so much?"

He kept talking. It was so hot here. I was hearing him and asking questions, but I wasn't listening to him.

I looked at him again. Then I thought: "This man is like my mother." Though she wasn't an addict, she had as many limitations as he did, as I did, as we all did. He had traded his daughter's safety by letting her mother terrorize her just so that he could satisfy his addiction. He and she, that wonderful mother, had their own evil contract: "I'll let you use your drugs and I'll use my terror." Maybe it wasn't that simple; but didn't my mother trade her life, and ours, for her own addiction to the chaos she and my father created? I had learned well. We had all traded, without even knowing it, our integrity and some essential part of ourselves. Why, I wondered. To combat loneliness? For excitement? To be a big shot? To simply stop the pain?

"How can I like him so much, and forgive him so fast for what he did, and still not forgive my mother?" Then I realized that the "whys" weren't as important as the "is's." If I insisted on knowing why, then I was playing God. And, of course, playing God in my tiny little world is what got me into so much trouble in the first place. So I let go of the "why's," and embraced the "is's." This guy is in pain. I've been in pain. My mother has lived her entire life in pain. Then I thought this is what Kimberly meant. The pain in inevitable. It is the misery which is chosen. I vowed and prayed that this moment would be the starting of the end of misery.

"Okay," I said to myself. "Liam, I don't care if what you said is crap. I don't care if the hugs are Oprahized and orchestrated. This must be the faith that Eddy sees in me that I don't. I am done with being miserable."

I looked back at Terry who was staring at his feet. I said: "You're from Georgia, right?"

He smiled that wonderful smile and said: "E-yup," stretching out his response as though he and I were talking on long-distance telephones with the signal being bounced off a far-flung satellite.

I looked at him and asked: "Can you tell me what that nutmeg Christmas smell is?

Resistance, Relapse, Denial and Death

A wild dog lived near the gates of the center. No one knew his real name but the staff called him "Relapse" so that was the name we all used. His eyes were covered by his fur, which was dark gray, stringy and tangled, like an old janitor's mop. His lower jaw did not fit his upper jaw. The lower was set over an inch or two, like he was clenching on a cigar.

We were prohibited from having contact with him because, according to the staff, he was wild. This meant no feeding, no food scraps thrown to him and no attempts at petting. Only God knew what diseases he might have. No one knew how old he was. One of the senior staff members said she knew he had to be at least ten years old because she had been there ten years, and that he had been there when she first arrived. There were many myths about Relapse. One was that if you saw him you were sure to relapse yourself. Another was that if you didn't see him you would easily relapse. All the patients loved him, especially Andy and the Professor. Andy couldn't start his day without seeing Relapse. If Andy didn't see him, he would spin a tale of what Relapse would be doing in the woods. On those days, the Professor would reassure Andy with the science of dog survival.

The area by the gate was, more or less, urban wild. There were lots of scrub growth trees and shrubs. The drive which intersected this growth was a black scar cutting through it. There was a small island of flowers at the beginning of the drive, which is where Relapse held court and where patients paid him homage.

The homage was simple: all the steaks, ribs and fast-food refuse of the patients were left in a pile in the flowers. All of the domes put their leftovers out for him. Relapse had learned to be picky. He would rarely eat the fast-food, preferring instead the high quality beef. Sometimes the other food grew rancid because he wouldn't eat it. When this happened, all the patients were assembled and once again told not to leave food for him. When the appeals to hygiene didn't work, the staff would use the Disney emotional appeal. What if a car hit him when he was trying to eat a takeout from Outback?

Karen especially commanded us to leave him to nature. "Jesus!" she screamed. "He's lived for at least ten years without you. The last thing he needs is a bunch of addicts thinking they can care from him. You can't even care for yourself! You're nothing more than his dealers! Leave him the fuck alone!"

The act of relapse was a constant threat to all of us. It was a daily struggle to stay "in recovery." The abandon represented by the culture of "sex, drugs and rock n' roll" was alluring. This attraction was actually increased when we shared the "high" points of our stories. Not too many talked about the consequences unless forced. Facing the consequences was painful, but it was necessary to stay sober.

Staff often told us that relapse was part of the disease. I wondered if this was a way of giving us permission to fuck up. When asked, Cliff, Karen, Kathy all said it was not permission. Instead, they said, it was a warning. It was a description of The Disease. Cliff said, "It's like having a heart attack and continuing to eat potato chips and ice cream. It's dumb and stupid, but we know lots of you are going to do it." Kathy once said: "It's not a moral issue. It's a health issue." Karen said: "It's fucking stupid."

We had people relapsing all the time, which scared the shit out of me. What if it happened to me? I'm not sure if the fear was irrational, but it was real. Few of us knew any more about the nature of relapse than we did about the science of addiction. We talked about relapses as if we were living in 14th century Europe and discussing the Plague. The nature of the disease was invisible, but the exploding boils weren't. I'm not sure if we were exchanging any valuable information, but in the world of relapse, Mondays were the best day since the relapses usually took place over the weekends.

The Rules were to keep us from relapsing, but those, of course, only worked if we wanted them to work. The "buddy" rule was the easiest to get around. The theory was that it was nearly impossible to get three people to go along with a lie, so whenever we were off campus there had to be at least three of us. Yet when people were similarly motivated, conspiracies were easy to maintain.

On one Monday, the relapse crisis-gossip centered around three guys from three different domes who had accompanied each other to an AA meeting off-campus. Their AA meeting took place at a prohibited strip club where Cherry Vanilla turned out to be an undercover cop just waiting to take advantage of poor guys in recovery who couldn't say a collective "no" to her singular "yes." Cherry's boa got in the way of a three-some arrest, so while two of them ran away, the third, who Cherry nicknamed "Turtle Dick" for physical reasons, wound up in her special overnight cell. Pam told me that he was into bondage and discipline so maybe it worked out well for him anyway. Back to the hospital for all of them. Later, Turtle Dick said that jail was better than the hospital. I thought he was crazy.

One of Pam's domemates was in a process of constant relapse. She was an owner of a pharmacy and had memorized scores of various and valid drug identification numbers of doctors. On Sunday mornings, she would call a large chain pharmacy and prescribe herself narcotics, using a different doctor's number each week. After spiritual and before lunch, she'd talk some of the other women patients into going through the drive-thru pick-up window of the pharmacy of the week. By dinner she had enough drugs to stay stoned for the week. She got caught when the DEA put a new computer program on the chain drug stores. The program signaled when any particular patient had a large number of prescriptions. The staff were extremely upset that no other patient had mentioned these regular Sunday pickups. Back to the hospital for them all.

The relapse I wish I had seen was on Christmas Eve when two guys smuggled in a half-gallon of vodka. They drank it and went to Father Liam's special Christmas Eve spiritual. They brought unwanted attention to themselves because they giggled every time he said "the baby Jesus." One of them, Doug, echoed Liam and said "the baby Jesus" in an exaggerated Southern minister fashion. Doug was very good looking. Even though he appeared straight, underneath he was not. He had told me he used to prostitute himself for crack cocaine. Once he had come into my apartment and made some moves on me. In my old life, I would have taken him home. In the beginning of my new life, I just got scared. I don't know what I would have done if I had been there that Christmas Eve. He was so nice, so good looking, so masculine and so fucked-up. My kind of guy. His mockery of Liam sent him back to the hospital and then out of treatment. The last I heard, Doug was sleeping with whomever he could find.

The Professor seemed to know more about relapse than the rest of the patients or even some of the staff. After Doug was kicked out of treatment, the Professor said: "You liked him, no?"

I was amazed that he could have seen that. "Yes," I answered, partially ashamed and intrigued at the same time. "How did you know that?"

The Professor laughed: "It is obvious when you like someone. You flirt with your humor and you are so very kind." He laughed again and said: "Not unlike me with the women! In fact, as I think about it, it is the same thing!"

I had never thought that my humor and kindness were seduction and told him so. He laughed again. "Ron, you are so American. If you were European, you would admit that all you are doing is attempting to satisfy a very primal need. There is nothing wrong with that."

"Professor," I said, "There was enough wrong with it for me to get arrested and wind up here."

"Bah," he said, "that's just your American Puritanism working overtime. If you were living in Europe, you would have no problems."

"That may be true," I said, "but I am living here, and I am having problems here. I can't even begin to think about living elsewhere. In fact, right now, I never want to leave treatment."

"Ah!" The Professor exclaimed, which he was always doing. "That is only because the staff loves you and pays constant attention to you."

"Well, whatever the reason, I like it."

"There will be a time when you must go home, no?: To face the courts and to go back to work?"

"Yeah," I said.

He asked: "Do you still mean what you said when you first came here?"

"What was that?" I asked.

"You said I don't care if I have to lose everything, I just don't want to be miserable anymore."

I thought for a moment. "Yeah," I said, "It's painful but at the same time it's a relief if it happens. Kathy thinks I planned all this just to get out of the crazy life I had created."

The Professor said: "She may be right. Kathy is wise, so unlike most Americans. But then I think she is partially Native American, which would explain her gifts. I am so attracted to her."

"Professor," I said, "she is staff. She's in the same position as a doctor. How can you think about fucking her?"

He laughed. "Of course I think about fucking her! She is a woman. Of course I would neither tell her about it nor do it."

I said: "Yeah, after all, she's got your license in her hands. Don't you think you should tell her? I mean, we're not supposed to have any secrets. Cliff keeps telling me 'You're only as sick as your secrets.' I'm dumping secrets left and right."

"Ah, Ron," he said with a mock look of stupefied superiority, "you are not only so American, you are so Catholic. You think confession will lead to absolution."

"I'm willing to try. Absolution would be nice."

"You Americans always think there is a second chance. That is where your 'born-agains' come from. If you were an older, more sophisticated culture, you would realize that people just are the way they are. There may be renewal, but there is no rebirth."

"So," I asked, "you're here just getting your batteries recharged?"

He laughed again, put a finger to his lips and said: "Shhh! Yes, of course, but don't tell anyone or they won't let me go!"

I said: "Should I tell Kathy you are 'Ever-ready?'"

Laughing, he walked away.

I went down the hall. There was a note on the board that all members of my dome were to meet in an hour for an "emergency meeting." I found Pam and asked her if she knew what the meeting was about. She said she didn't know for sure but it was something about Andy. She and I were talking when a woman patient came up to her and said: "I've got to drop. Can you take my urine?"

Pam and I both started laughing. "Where else," she said, "would that be normal language? I'll find you after your meeting."

I worried about Andy. I hadn't seen him since I left the apartment, but that wasn't unusual. He was always late. He skipped groups sometimes and just laid in the sun or in the corners of unused rooms. I walked through the building and then again outside but couldn't find him.

I went into the room where the emergency meeting was going to be held. There were already a few other domemates there, including Brand and the Professor. They apparently had been arguing about something.

Brand said to him: "You are so sick!"

The Professor said: "Ask Ron, he too witnessed it."

"Witnessed what?" I asked.

The Professor said: "The addict masturbating himself at the gas station."

"Yeah," I said. "We sure saw that."

About a week earlier, Andy, the Professor and I stopped at a nearby gas station so I could put gas in my car. The place was always full of patients and street people. The only reason the staff let us use it was because it was the closest gas station to campus. I went in to pay for gas and missed most of it, but when I came out, Andy said: "Look, Ron! Your kind of guy." Then he pointed to a young man talking on a pay phone while rubbing his crotch.

"What do you think he's doing?" Andy asked.

The Professor said: "Andy, you are so silly. He's playing with himself while talking to a connection." As we watched, a spot formed in the front of the guy's jeans. It got bigger and turned a dark shade of blue. The spot kept expanding.

Andy said: "C'mon Ron, go over there and ask if he's got any left for you."

I got so mad. "Andy, why do you insist on always reminding me of who I was, where I was. Don't you believe in change or that any of this experience is worthwhile."

"C'mon, Ron," he said, "don't get so upset. None of us will change. We are the way we are. We're just in camp right now. You'll always be addicted to sex, drugs and rock 'n roll. We all are. You're the only one who insists that there is a better you somewhere."

As we drove away, Andy kept laughing. I wouldn't talk with

him. He said: "C'mon Ron. You're not so different from us or that guy. He just jacks off in public. So what? I used to do it in school under the desk. A bunch of us would jack off under our desks while looking at this young teacher we had. Female, of course, you fag."

I was so mad at him. "Andy, did you ever stop to think that jacking off with a bunch of other guys was just a little gay?"

"Nope," he said, "we were looking at a girl. You look at guys. That makes you a fag."

"Thanks for the definition, Andy," I said. "You've saved me from a lifetime of wondering."

"Stop it, gentlemen," said the Professor. "I wonder if the two of you realize you're just a little in love with each other. Andy is afraid of the love because of his own sexual conflicts. Ron is afraid of it because he realizes that you, Andy, are a borderline personality and, to use a Ron quote, 'the better angels of his nature' are attempting to take over. After all, Andy, as cute and smart as you may be, you are still very crazy."

Andy laughed and said: "Professor, you are so right."

More patients walking into the room brought me back into the present. There was some small talk, then Kathy walked in with Cliff, who had his omnipresent clipboard and pen. Brand looked at them and turned white. I wondered if he had done something or was just so terrified of their authority that he got scared no matter what.

Kathy closed the door, looked around and said: "Let's do an attendance check-in."

With the exception of Andy, we were all there. The door opened and Karen walked in. Three senior members of staff? This must be serious.

As she sat down, she said: "okay, who has seen Andy today?"

No one spoke. Everyone looked at me. I said: "I saw him when I left the dome to come here."

Karen said: "When was that?"

"About 8:30," I said.

"Doesn't he usually ride with you?" she asked.

"Yes, but today he said he wanted to walk over. He said he thought his chances of seeing Relapse were greater if he weren't in a car."

"He never showed up," Karen said.

"So what?" I asked. "He's probably sleeping somewhere."

Brand said: "He's always skipping and sleeping in."

Karen said: "He's not in the dome."

Brand said: "Then he's dead somewhere. Who cares?"

Cliff's face got red. "Brand, you just got put on restriction."

Brand turned white again. "For what? He's an asshole. You only care for him because you know Ron likes him and Ron's your favorite."

Karen said: "Enough of that. Keep going Brand, and you'll wind up in the hospital for hostility."

Kathy coughed and said: "We went to his apartment. All of his belongings are neatly packed and have been placed on his bed. He left a note, which I want to read: "I'll come back later for my stuff. I have two of Ron's CDs and three of Doug's. The Professor has $300 of mine he's been holding which I'll want. Don't worry, I'm not going to do anything too stupid. I'm going to contact some of my friends here and get started again. Don't call my dad."

None of us said anything.

Cliff asked: "Okay? What's happened that we don't know about? Why would he want to leave?"

We all stayed silent. Cliff said: "Brand, did you say anything to him?"

Brand gasped: "Me? Why would I say anything to that fag lover?"

I was so tired of this, but I started to say something anyway. Cliff interrupted and said: "Brand, do you want us to talk about your sex life right now?"

Brand turned crimson. "No sir," he said.

"Well then," Cliff said, "shut the fuck up with your denial and your criticisms. We need information."

Kathy said: "We're reading this as a suicide note. We have called Andy's dad."

"He hates his dad," I said.

Kathy looked at me with her deep brown eyes. "Ron, we know that. We know the issues. But he still has a father who cares about him. Now, what's happened?"

I sat there saying nothing while everyone stared at me. Cliff started tapping his pen against his clipboard.

"Nothing major happened. Just this little deal at the gas station last week." I told them what happened. "I didn't think it was that big a deal. I get mad at him all the time."

Cliff said: "You didn't see that as an invitation from him for sex?"

"No," I said. "He's always talking like that."

Kathy, Cliff and Karen then looked at the Professor.

Cliff said: "Professor, with all your education and accomplishments, didn't you realize you were pushing Andy into a conflict with himself which he had been using drugs to deal with?"

The Professor, who was always aware that staff had his financial future in their collective hands, said: "Well, what I said was just a comment. It was just a remark. It was not a psychological bromide."

Karen said: "We don't have time for this discussion shit. Professor, why do you have $300 of Andy's money? You know the rules. None of you are allowed to have more than $30 at any time.

The Professor was silent. Cliff said: "Professor, you've got the same look on your face that Brand does just before he lies."

Karen said: "Professor, you're on restriction."

The Professor said: "But I'm due to be discharged next week!"

Karen said: "Until this is cleared up, you will not be discharged. You are on restriction until further notice."

The Professor started to say something, but Karen stood up and said: "I don't have time for this crap. We can't rescue you from yourselves unless you're here, and you still have to be open, honest and willing. Doesn't sound to me like you're any of those. If you can't obey our little rules here, in this controlled community, what makes you think you can obey the rules when no one is watching?"

The Professor started to say something again. Karen looked directly at him and said: "You want to talk? Then come with me when I call Andy's dad and try to explain why we – why none of us – know where he is or if he's dead or alive. You want to teach me how to do that, Professor?"

The Professor said nothing, nor did he move. Karen looked around the room once, like she was the Wicked Witch looking for Dorothy in disguise. I had just learned that she wasn't a witch at all. She was powerless and she knew it. She was scared. She jerked the door open and slammed it as she left.

No one moved or said anything. Kathy and Cliff were trained to handle silences. Brand started to move around and Cliff glared at him.

After a minute, Cliff said: "Here are the rules. If Andy contacts any of you, you are to immediately contact one of the staff. If it's after hours, you are to call the counselor-on-call. You are not to engage him in conversation beyond finding out where he is and reassuring him that he is always welcome back here. You are not to call him, meet him, or offer him any assistance. Any questions?"

No one had any. Cliff and Kathy stood up. The patients started for the door and Cliff said: "Whoa. Wait a second. Let's form a circle. If we ever needed the Serenity Prayer, we need it now."

We all formed a circle, arms on each other. Kathy led the Prayer. As I walked out, Kathy touched my arm. "Just a minute," she said.

I looked at her and said: "What?" I had that feeling that I always had when someone in authority wanted to talk to me when I wasn't prepared. The room emptied of patients but Cliff stayed back with her.

She looked at me and asked: "Do you have any idea where he is?"

I looked back and immediately said: "No. None." I thought for another moment and said: "Wait. There's that gas station where the addicts hang out." They both shook their heads up and down.

"Yeah," Cliff said, "that's the first place we check. Not there, and no one has seen him."

I said: "There's also an abandoned house near there. Andy was always talking about how he'd like to restore it and then all of us and our dogs could live there." Cliff made a note.

"Okay," he said. "I've got to go."

As I followed him and Kathy out the door, she looked at me and said: "You know, none of this is your fault."

"I know that," I said.

She said: "Yeah."

I said: "okay. I was feeling guilty."

She chuckled and said: "I know. You wouldn't be you if you didn't."

Tears immediately welled up in both my eyes. I looked in her eyes. They were so dark, so deep. "Do I ever get over this?" I asked.

She looked at me, nodded and said: "Yes. You do. Did you meet Andy's dad when he was here?"

I said: "Yeah. I had dinner with them. Remember? You guys had to give me permission."

She smiled. "Yes. I remember. Well, then, your head knows what's going, doesn't it?"

I stood still and answered slowly: "Yes." My head sure did know. That dinner was one of the most bizarre meals I had ever shared. His dad charmed the wait staff and worked on charming me, but there was no connection between Andy and his dad except well-disguised hatred.

Kathy looked at me and said: "Then you know. You need to learn to trust your gut as much as you do your head."

I kept looking at her eyes. "Andy's relapse is a lesson for me too, isn't it?" I laughed and said: "Even with all your concern and fear about him, you're doing therapy on me right now aren't you?"

She smiled and said: "Ron, part of trusting yourself also means not having to say everything you know." She touched the tip of my nose with the tip of her finger and walked away.

I walked outside to my car. The Professor was standing next to it. He very angrily said to me: "Well, now that I am on restriction, I must be accompanied by a trusted senior addict such as yourself. Would you please give me a ride to my residence?"

"Professor," I said, "your sarcasm isn't going to do us any good. And the rule is that you are to be accompanied by two senior addicts, so we'd better find someone else to ride with us."

"Baah," he said, as he walked back into the building.

Andy's disappearance was the only topic at the dome. I went to bed early but was awakened by one of my roommates at about 11:00 p.m.

"Ron," he said, "telephone." Then he whispered: "I think it's Andy." I went out to the living room.

It was Andy. His voice was high-pitched. "Hey, man, what's going on?"

I immediately got angry. All my roommates were looking at me.

"Andy," I asked, "Where are you?"

He laughed: "I'm not telling you, because you'll tell staff."

"That's exactly right," I said. "Now stop this bullshit. Everyone wants you back."

"No," he said, "they don't want me. They just want my money."

"Andy, they really do want you back. Just tell me where you are."

"No, Ron." He was quiet for a moment. "You're going to call staff as soon as we hang up, aren't you?"

"Yes, which will be in about two seconds" I answered.

He cackled: "You'll never find me. Your dogs might, but you won't." Then he hung up.

I immediately called the counselor-on-call and related the phone call. The counselor took the information and said: "Don't go back to bed right away. One of the senior staff members will be calling you."

Five minutes later the phone rang again. It was Karen. I told her what I had already told the counselor.

Karen said: "What do you think he meant about your dogs finding him?"

I answered: "I don't know. He knows how much I love my dogs. He talks about them all the time. He talks about how they and Relapse could live in the woods while Andy, Kevin and I live in that abandoned house by the gas station. Just silly shit."

"No fucking shit it's silly!" she said. Then, "Ah, I'm sorry. I shouldn't be yelling at you. You know, Andy's only about three years old emotionally. His idea of the perfect relationship is probably that of a dog and his owner. To him it probably seems that the dog is free, which to Andy means that he gets to do what he wants to do. He doesn't see that the dog is dependent upon the human for food and care."

"Except for Relapse," I said.

"Except for Relapse," she said, "but Relapse still takes the food you guys leave for him. And Relapse is not a pet."

"Neither is Andy," I said.

"Listen," she said, "it's too fucking late for these kinds of conversations. Call us when he calls back."

"Don't you mean 'if?'" I asked.

"Jesus! You are so fucking blind sometimes! Of course he's going to call you back! You're the only human he talks to!" With that, she hung up. I went back to bed.

I didn't fall asleep right away. I kept wondering about the Relapse connection and the symbolism. Later, I heard the phone ring again. I got up, ran into the living room and answered it: "Hello?"

"Hey, man," Andy said. He sounded so peaceful. His voice was still high-pitched, but he was articulate. "You know why I left?"

"Yeah," I said. "You wanted to get fucked up."

He didn't answer. I asked: "Where are you?"

He laughed: "I'm with the dogs looking for the Professor."

"Where is that?" I asked. I was starting to get pissed. He wasn't making any sense. He wouldn't make any sense while he was this fucked up. He was reminding me of my father when he was fucked up: Beautiful, meaningless, cryptic sentences.

Andy said: "Have fun calling the staff." Then he hung up.

I called the counselor and related the conversation. Less than a minute later Karen called me back. She asked: "Where's the Professor?"

I said: "I have no idea. He doesn't live in this apartment." She was silent for a moment. "You're right," she said, as though I could have been wrong about the identity of the people I lived with. "Hang on. I'm going to call his apartment on my mobile phone!"

There was silence for a moment. Then I heard her scream: "What the goddamn fuck do you mean he's not in his room! Jesus fucking Christ!"

She came back on the line with me: "Listen. Stay there. Stay awake. Stay near the phone." With that she hung up.

I went into my room, took the bedspread off the bed, grabbed a pillow and made a bed on the couch.

As I was falling asleep, I didn't really wonder where the Professor was. I knew. He was out spending Andy's money, either with Andy or without him. Andy would be mad if the Professor was spending the money alone. Andy loved money. He loved saving it and hated spending it.

The phone rang again. It was Andy.

"Hey man," he said. His voice was lower now and a little more tired.

"Hey," I said.

"Did you call the staff?" he asked.

"You know I did," I answered.

"Yeah, Ron, the good little gay boy, pleasing everyone so they will please him." He purposefully exaggerated my name. "Raw-uh-on."

"You know why I left?" he asked.

"You already asked me that one. Yeah, to get fucked up. Congratulations. It sounds like you've succeeded in your quest."

"Naw. It was because I was going to have to start paying for treatment."

I was surprised. "What do you mean," I asked, "weren't you paying for it?"

"No," he said. "My dad was, but then he said he wouldn't anymore because I wasn't getting well enough fast enough."

"So what," I said, "you've got your own money." I knew that Andy had saved and inherited enough money to pay for treatment twice over, which I told him.

He angrily said: "That's for my retirement!"

I laughed and said: "You're not even 30! And you won't make it to retirement if you keep fucking up like this. Your dad will inherit your money."

He said: "Fuck that. Where's the Professor?"

"Andy," I said, "I don't know. And I'm not supposed to talk to you except to ask where you are and to tell you that you are welcome to return."

"But I want to tell you something," he said. There was a long silence. "I want to tell you how much I love you."

I froze. Then he giggled and hung up.

I called the counselor. Karen called right back. "Okay," she said. "That's it for the game playing. Go to bed. If he calls back, don't talk to him. Don't engage him in conversation. He knows your buttons. Get some sleep." Then she hung up without saying goodbye.

I laid down on the couch and actually fell asleep. I heard the phone ringing through the pillow, which I had pulled over my head.

I stood up and stumbled over the other phone: "Hello?" I said. It was Andy.

"Hey man," he said.

I looked at the clock on the stove. It was 5:40 a.m. I didn't say anything.

Andy said: "Ah, c'mon Ron, I know you're there."

"Where are you Andy?"

He sounded very tired. "I'm with Relapse. Hey! I'm relapsing with Relapse."

"Andy," I said. "I'm too tired for games. Tell me where you are or I'm hanging up."

He said: "okay. I'm at the gas station at the pay phone. I was with Relapse, though. That fucking Professor was supposed to meet me to give me my money and the fucker never showed up. Hey! Ron! Relapse has friends!"

"What," I asked.

"Relapse has friends. I went into the woods and followed him. I hid in the bushes. There are about five dogs that hang out together in the woods. Relapse is their leader. They all do what he says. But they run, and hunt, and eat, and sleep together. It is so cool back there."

As he was speaking, I remembered when he told me about loving the beautiful, iridescent snake and how he smashed it's head.

"Andy," I said, "you haven't hurt Relapse, have you?"

"Ron, no, never," he said. "But I realize that he and his dog friends all love each other. And I love you too. Your dogs can live with Relapse and we can live in that old house."

"Andy," I said, "that will never happen. It's absurd to even think like that."

"Ron," he said, "I bet you would if I gave you this present I've got for you."

"Andy, what the fuck are you talking about?"

"My dick, Ron, it's so hard right now. I was thinking about girls, and then I thought about the Professor, and then I thought I'd let you suck it. It would be so cool. You can meet me now. I'll show you where Relapse lives."

I froze again. It felt like a hook was going into my soul. As I started to talk, it felt like Cliff and Kathy were in my head talking to me.

"Andy," I said, "If I thought you were honest about this, I'd be tempted. I'd be more than tempted. But you're just fucked up."

"No, man, I mean it," he said. "It's been hard thinking about you. I want you to do this. It's a big present!" Then he giggled.

I don't know how I did it, but I said, "Goodbye, Andy."

"Don't hang up, man! The sun is just coming up. It will be beautiful: You, me, and the dogs."

I was paralyzed. I had so many thoughts. My father, my family, my friends, my aloneness and my own anger. I hung up. I looked outside. The sun was coming up. It was red behind the pine trees. 'Red in the morning, sailors take warning.' Clichés always came to me in times of crisis. I went to the couch, wrapped myself in the bedspread and looked out the window. When I was a kid, I used to memorize powerful songs to use when I died and my soul was in transition. I used to think that reciting the lyrics of "I Am The Walrus" or "Like A Rolling Stone" or singing a Gershwin or Porter love melody would keep the demons away. There were no lightning bolts, no flashes of light. There were no thunderous sounds, but I was just as scared as if there were. The demons weren't waiting for me after I died, they were there now. I felt so alone. I started crying.

I sat there for about half an hour and then called the counselor-on-call. She put me on hold, came back and said: "Senior staff is already on campus. Just go in at your normal time and they'll talk to you then."

There was a note on the board for me when I got on campus. It said: "See Kathy immediately."

I went to her office, but she wasn't there. Pam walked by and said: "Hey Love, what's up?"

I said: "I don't know, really. The Professor and Andy are both missing. Andy was playing phone games all night."

She looked at me with concern. "You haven't heard?"

"Heard what?" I asked.

"A patient died last night."

I panicked. "Andy?" I asked.

Pam said: "None of us know. Some cops are with senior staff in the conference room. I felt miserable. If it was Andy, would he be alive if I had taken up his invitation?

Pam said: "C'mon, let's go outside."

I'm supposed to see Kathy," I said.

"She'll find you." With that, Pam took my hand and led me outside. We sat in the sunshine. She smoked a cigarette.

"That'll kill you, ya' know?" I said. She smiled and said: "Yep."

We sat in silence. I thought how lucky I was to have friends like her. I hadn't known her more than a few months, but we had been through a war together. I told her what happened last night. I put my arm around her and said: "Pam, I feel like we're English pilots in the

Battle of Britain. We all try to fly to save ourselves and our country, but so many of us crash and die."

Pam looked at me, laughed and said: "Jesus! Doesn't that head of yours ever stop working? You are so good at romanticizing and distancing. Listen, Andy is a very sick guy who is, or maybe was, in love with you. But it really isn't love. The sexual come-on stuff is the only way he knows how to communicate. He's funny, charming, wickedly smart, but very, very sick."

She went on: "It's okay that he loves you. It's even okay if you want to love him back. And I'm sure he was very tempting last night. But the good news is that you didn't follow him. You let Cliff, Kathy and Karen and whatever else into your head and heart. You listened. You know there's a lot more to love than getting your cock sucked. And you're not alone. Jeez! When I think of the things I used to do!"

We laughed, because I knew some of those things. I loved her more because she had shared them, not as enticements or advertisements but instead as statements of who she had been. She had trusted me. I told her that. She looked at me and said: "

"Trust is love too." Of course, I started to cry again.

Pam said: "You must have one hell of a higher power. He gives you just what you need when you need it. And he gives you the gift of being able to understand it."

Kathy walked out at that point. She said: "Hello. Pam, all of the patients are assembling in the auditorium. You need to go in there."

Pam and I stood up. Kathy said: "Ron, come with me. You can skip the beginning of the meeting."

I went with Kathy into her office. The only reason to separate us, I thought, was to tell me that Andy had died. When we sat down, I said: "Is Andy dead?"

She looked at me with those incredibly dark eyes. Tears started to form around them, but it was me that started to cry.

"No," she said. "Andy is back down at the hospital. He came in right after your last call with him."

I said: "But Pam said she had heard that a patient died last night."

"Yes," Kathy said. She leaned forward, towards me, put her hand on my knee and said: "It wasn't Andy. It was the Professor."

I was stunned. "The Professor?"

"Yes," she said. "We're still not sure of all the details. The police are still investigating. Right now we know very little. But apparently he was supposed to meet with Andy to give him his money back. Instead, the Professor bought some drugs from a woman at the gas station. According to the police, she says they were only going to have sex. He either overdosed or reacted to whatever it is he took. They found his body about an hour ago. It was behind the gas station. Karen is meeting with all the patients right now. That's what the meeting is about."

I didn't know what to say. We sat in silence. Kathy said: "Ron, there are some people so hurt that their wounds can't be nursed."

"Are you talking about the Professor or Andy?" I asked.

She shrugged and said nothing, as though it was up to me to figure it out.

I said: "I probably shouldn't say this, but you didn't see what we saw. And nice, highly functioning people die from the disease every day. The nature of the disease is to be deceptive."

I asked: "Can I see Andy?"

She smiled and said: "Yes. You can see him now. I'm not sure he's going to want to come back."

"Why not?" I said. "He will die otherwise!"

She smiled and shrugged again.

"Ron," she said, "sometimes there are no answers. I know that doesn't appeal to you because you think everything can be figured out. Sometimes the 'why' is much less important than the 'what.' Even if we figure out all the 'whys,' the 'whats' still exist. And the 'whats' can really hurt us."

"If you want to see Andy, you'd better go now. He's going to meet with us all in an hour and he might not like the restrictions he'll be put on if he stays."

I started to ask what restrictions. She said: "You're not his lawyer. This is not a court. You're his friend. Go be a friend."

I said: "Can I see you after I see him?"

She said: "Sure."

I walked down to the hospital. The tennis shoes were still hanging on the wires. The sun was warm. The nutmeg was still on the path.

Kathy must have called ahead. I was let right into the lock-down ward. Andy had been in his room and was escorted to the visitor's area by a hospital staff member.

"Ya'll have about half an hour, I'd guess," the staff member told us.

Andy looked terrible. He had on the exact same outfit he had on the first day I had seen him lying on the grass, glittering in the sunshine. He was filthy. There were bits of dead, dried leaves in his hair. His face had patchy bits of red, like he had been picking zits. There were cuts on his hands. His neck had a huge bruise.

"So," I said, "been doing anything interesting recently?"

He scowled at me and said nothing.

I waited in silence. I was mad at him; Mad for scaring me; Mad because the Professor had just died while waiting for him; Mad for trying to pick me up; Mad for neither of us living an honest life.

I said: "Picked up any interesting men?"

He turned red. "Listen," he said, "I didn't say what you said I said."

"Oh," I said, "Already met with the staff have you? You're going to try and rewrite the truth?"

He said: "Just because someone says something when they're fucked up doesn't mean they mean it."

I didn't know what to do. But I remembered something the Professor had said about the "better angels of my nature."

"Andy," I said, "I would have loved to have been with you, but not fucked up."

He smiled and said, "Ah, c'mon Ron, you know you would have."

I said nothing. I looked at him. He wasn't glistening now.

"Andy," I said, "maybe I would have, but I didn't."

I stood up and said: "I've got to go. I want to see if I can go to the Professor's funeral."

Andy smiled an endearing smile and said: "Ah, c'mon. We've

still got some time."

I smiled back, shook my head and said: "No, I've got to go now. I'll see you up the hill."

Andy's smile turned into a frown. He said: "I don't know about that."

I laughed: "Oh, Andy, it's only money. Jesus! Get rid of your money and get a life!"

"Look who's talking," he said.

"Yeah, I know, it's trapped me too," I said. "But I'm willing to learn otherwise. I'll see you later."

Andy stood and said: "I'm not sure that you will."

I said, "Well, that's up to you."

He walked towards me. I put my arms out and we hugged. He whispered in my ear: "I'm so sorry, Ron. I'm so sorry."

I was amazed, again. Why should he be sorry? I turned my head to look at him. He was crying. He put his lips on my neck and kissed me. He kept crying. I grasped his head, pulled it to mine and touched his forehead with mine.

I looked around the visitor's room. "Andy," I said, "Look at this place. It's clean, the magazines are new and there are windows. But can't you smell the misery?"

He didn't say anything.

"Andy," I said. "I want to get out of this, but the right way. I'm tired of running from myself. I want to break this trap. I am tired of walking on wires. I am tired of the misery. It's time for me to go home."

He whispered against my ear: "But you'll go to jail."

"I know," I said, "and I am scared about that. But that will only be painful. It won't be miserable unless I make it that way. Andy, I don't want to be a broken hero."

I stood back from him. He got a dark look on his face and said: "If you tell anyone about this, I'll kill you."

I laughed and said: "No you won't."

Andy's face changed again. He smiled a little and his eyes glistened. He said: "I told you about Relapse, didn't I? That he has a home hidden in the woods and that he has dog friends?" He stood taller. "One of them is a big shepherd, bigger than he is, but Relapse is still the boss."

I hugged him again and said: "Yeah, Andy, I know he is."

With that, I smiled and walked back up to the hill.

Cliff Makes a Miracle

I constantly worried about the future. Every scenario I could think of scared the shit out of me. I wanted my old life back. In exchange, I promised the excess would be gone; that I would behave; that I would appreciate what I had; that I would learn the difference between needs and wants. I'm not sure how sincere the promises were, but the fear was real. In my more clear moments, I remembered the prayer I had made while in my suicide cell: "God, please let me die. Please let me die." It took me so long to realize the prayer was granted the moment I said it. There was no way I could have my old life back. It was dead. The old "I" was dead.

Cliff stopped me in the hall. "Hey," he said, "what's this I hear about you not talking in groups?"

"What?" I said. "I talk all the time." I started to give him examples of recent group talk. He put his hand on my shoulder and said: "I know your mouth has been moving. I don't think that could ever stop. It's the way you are talking, or aren't talking. You're not saying anything. You're simply being charming and entertaining."

I thought: "What's wrong with that? What more is there?"

"Cliff," I said, "we were just talking about fear in Kathy's group. And how can you say that I've got a problem if I talk or don't talk? That's a little inconsistent. Logically…"

He tightened his hand on my shoulder. "Ron," he said, "don't give me your logic. This is not a courtroom. It's also not a cocktail party or a political fundraiser. I'm sure that back home you could divert attention from yourself by your techniques. They don't work here. We don't want them to work here. You don't want them to work here."

"Who are you to say if what I'm saying is valuable or honest?" I asked him.

He started laughing. "I'm your therapist! I'm the guy who knows how to separate your shit from your bullshit. I'm the guy who's going to save your life. And your charming, political cocktail talk is a retreat. You're going into yourself again. You're romancing suicide."

The fear hit me as he said that. He was right. I was falling asleep thinking of how to die, quietly, without fanfare. In groups when I was talking, I was actually thinking of death. It was seductive. Earlier there had been a cop in the building. I walked behind him and started to reach out my hand to grab his gun. I had done that as though I was on automatic. I would have grabbed it except that he walked out of my reach. I thought death was freedom. I told Cliff this.

He said: "You know what would have happened?"

I said, "I would have killed myself."

He laughed: "That cop would have grabbed your arm, shoved you to the ground and dislocated your shoulder. Then you would have gone to jail and stayed there for a while."

"I'm going to go to jail anyway," I said.

"Oh," he said, "so now you're going to give me the 'whatever' response? That's bullshit and you know it. Are you in jail now?"

"Well, this could be considered a jail and..."

"Stop it." Cliff said: "Come with me." With that, he guided me down the hall toward the "staff only" door. The door was glass and sunlight was coming through it. Even though it was winter up north, it was warm in Georgia. He placed me next to the door.

"Where are you now?" he asked.

I thought this was absurd. I had no idea what he meant. I said: "I'm standing in the hallway of a psychiatric hospital in Georgia."

"Okay," he said. "Where aren't you?"

I had no idea what he meant and said nothing. He opened the door, grabbed my arm, led me outside and placed me directly in the sunlight.

"Where are you now?" he asked.

"I am standing in the sunlight on the sidewalk next to the "staff only" glass door of a psychiatric facility in Georgia."

He smiled and said: "Where aren't you?"

I had no idea what he was getting at. He smiled, grabbed my arm and led me back inside. "Where are you now?"

I said: "What the fuck is this? I have no idea what you're talking about." He just smiled and took me outside again. Still smiling, he took me inside again. Then he placed his foot in the corner of the door leaving it open and led me back and forth. We both started laughing.

"Okay, okay," I said. "I'm not where I was a moment ago."

"That's right," he said. He stopped moving me. "Where else aren't you?"

I was bewildered. He stopped laughing and said: "You're not in a coffin. You're not in jail."

"So?" I said. I'll be in both soon enough."

He said: "You know your problem?"

I said: "Yeah, listening to you."

He led me outside again. The sunlight felt good. It felt great.

Cliff said: "Do you believe in UFOs?"

I was surprised by the question. "UFOs? I don't think that's a matter of 'belief.' I think there's plenty of evidence to support their existence."

He smiled: "Spoken like a lawyer. Do you believe in miracles?"

"Cliff," I said, "your religion is showing."

He stopped smiling. "Ron, you know we talk about you a lot. I've got to admit there are things about you that don't make sense. On most things, you are like the Rock of Gibraltar. There is almost nothing you can't handle, but there are a few things that send cracks to your foundation so easily. I could say a few things that would place you back in the hospital in minutes."

I got scared. But I trusted him so much, even loved him, and wanted to trust him all the time. My face gave me away.

"I'm not going to do that. I just wanted you to know there is such strength in you. There is such tremendous faith."

"Yeah, well I don't see that."

"That's one of the things that makes those fissures so dangerous. Let me think." He really said that. "Let me think." He stared at my face. It was like watching Sherlock Holmes examine a clue.

He asked: "Why do you think the staff and the patients like you so much?"

"Do they?"

"C'mon. Don't be cute. You know they do."

"Well, probably because I charm them."

"Actually," he said, "That's one of the more disagreeable things about you."

Disagreeable? "Cliff, I've gone out of my way to learn how to charm people."

He laughed, "Yeah, we know that. It's obvious. You are a master of the deeply superficial relationship. Most people think you're being real with them when you are simply using charm as an offense and a defense."

"Cliff, where is this going?"

"Ron, they like you because you make them feel good. You make the other patients feel safe."

"Well, I sure don't know I'm doing that."

"That's another reason."

This was too much for me. "Cliff, you're driving me nuts." He started laughing again. "Yeah, yeah," I said. "I know. I'm already nuts. That's why I'm here."

"No," he said. "You're here because you had a breakdown. And I'm here helping you to make that a breakthrough."

I said nothing. There was something about what he said that felt as though it made sense, but I couldn't work it out. He stared at my face again.

"Stop thinking. Let's get back to miracles."

I started getting mad. "Cliff, I will not discuss religion with you. It's all bullshit."

"Ron, it's not religion I'm offering. It's spirituality. I can show you a miracle right now. I'll even bet you on that."

"Okay," I said. "If you can't, then I get to stay here for free."

"All right," he said. "Come with me."

We left the building and walked across the parking lot down the hill. It was so warm. The leaves were still green. We said nothing as we walked. I thought of the soldiers from the North who must have been so hot in their wool uniforms when they marched through Georgia. What kept them going when they must have been so uncomfortable?

Cliff said: "What are you thinking about?"

I told him. He said: "Maybe they believed in miracles."

"Jeez, Cliff, probably they believed in Sherman, or Lincoln, or the abolition of slavery, or maybe they just believed they could get home if they did their job."

We had reached the bottom of the hill. He led me into the middle of the road. The tennis shoes were still hung, perfectly balanced, on the telephone wire.

He said: "Do you think Jesus walked on water?"

I started getting angry. "Cliff, I told you, none of this religious crap."

"Well," he said, "do you think any man or woman can walk on water?"

"Cliff, this is fifth grade Catholic crap. Yes, when it's frozen. But then it's ice and not water. Trick questions are not miracles."

He put his arm around my shoulder. I felt so safe when he did that. He led me about six feet. I felt as though I could walk with him forever. We stopped.

"You just walked across water."

"Cliff, what are you talking about? We just walked on pavement across a ditch."

"Yeah," he said, "but under that drainage ditch is a river which still flows. When Sherman's men walked through here, they had to walk through it. What we are doing would be a miracle to them. Minor perhaps, but still a miracle."

I started to argue but he put his arm on me again and walked me the other way. He led me back and forth until I started laughing.

"Okay! Okay!" I said. "It's a fucking miracle."

He said: "Where aren't you?"

I said: "I'm not in the river."

"That's right," he said. Then he asked: "Where else aren't you?"

"I'm not in jail."

"Where else aren't you?"

"I'm not in a coffin."

"And where else?" he asked.

This time, I stared at his face. I thought for a moment and said: "I'm not everywhere else. I'm not on the moon, in Paris, or flying around the sun."

"Where are you?"

I thought again. This was not a trick question. "For this moment," I said, "and maybe only for this moment, I am walking across water that would have stopped other people. I am with you in the sunshine, wanting to be here and loving being here. Okay, I'll grant you this little miracle."

"What's the real miracle?"

I was willing to give him his little 'walking across water' miracle but what did this mean, the 'real miracle?'

He smiled. I looked up at the tennis shoes on the wires and

thought of the effort it took to put them there. I looked into his face. I felt the warmth of the sun. I felt such a connection to him, to the warmth and to the person who put the shoes on the wires.

"The real miracle is that I trust you enough to walk this path."

He hugged me, put his arm around me, led me back up the hill and said: "It's all in the mind. It's all about perception."

We separated when we got back to campus. I had some time before I had to go to my next group, which was the lawyers' group, so I went into the lounge. Pam was there with Robbie, one of the rich kids. They were having an active conversation, so I just sat on one of the couches.

There was heat in her voice as she said: "Robbie, you are so spoiled! Your dad gave you a million dollars to see if you could do something with it, and all you did was hire limousines, whores and drug friends!"

He laughed at her and said: "Yeah, but I sure had fun!"

She said: "Just because you come from a rich family doesn't mean you don't have to be responsible."

Robbie hated it whenever his family's wealth was thrown up. He said: "Well, it's not like he's that rich. It's not like he's Bill Gates."

"Just take away a zero," Pam said.

I had to get in on this. "A zero?" I said. "Are you saying Robbie's a zero or that his dad is?"

Pam said: "No, take away a zero from Bill Gate's net worth to figure what Robbie's dad is worth. So instead of being a super-billionaire, his dad is just a regular billionaire."

Robbie had been living my dream. He had been handed a

million dollars, just to see what he'd do with it! I wondered if I would have done anything differently. I thought I probably would have not hired limousines because I liked to drive too much. I told Robbie and Pam that.

He said: "Yeah, me too, but I lost my license." He said this with a grin, but then he added: "That was really unfair."

Pam got angry, but I just laughed. I had this wonderful feeling of being set just right. It wasn't just clarity. It was a sense of sureness that I never had before. Robbie's reality had been my fantasy. It hadn't worked for him. He was there with me. For the first time, I emotionally realized that the million dollar dream was worthless. In reality, it wasn't a dream and it was worse than a nightmare. Pam and Robbie kept arguing about money. They reminded me of my parents.

I left the lounge and went into my group room. No one was there yet. I sat in a chair close to the door. Some new patients, who were usually the only ones on time, came in. None of them said anything but each looked at his schedule, walked into the hallway, looked at the room number and came back in. Each walked around the room like a dog trying to find a safe place to call his own. Lawyers like to know the rules. They love code books. I said nothing. This was too good and too enjoyable to interrupt.

Other current patients came in, sat down and started talking. The new patients started asking questions and then arguing with the answers they were given. I started smiling. All the patients sat down and we waited for the therapist who ran the group. He was not a lawyer, but instead was a psychologist who specialized more in collecting statistics about lawyers than in treating them. He was a nice guy, but boring. Not much normally happened in lawyers' group.

He didn't come into the room at all. Instead, a therapist named Guy walked in and sat down next to me. I didn't know him very well. He was older, fat, and had skin that looked like someone had stuck spackling compound on, leaving it to dry without sanding it. All I knew about him was that his patients either loved him or hated him. He treated many of them harshly, calling them names and humiliating them. He made one of them wear a sign that said: "I say stupid things so I can't talk until I say something smart." Whenever he walked by Andy, he looked at him and said: "Liar." Andy loved it. I would have hated it.

Guy said: "I'm handling the group tonight because, well, I don't know why. I was just told to be here, so here I am. I understand we have some new people here, so why don't we all introduce ourselves."

As each person did that, Guy smiled, nodded his head and said: "Welcome." One of the new patients had the same last name as a recent controversial president.

Guy asked him: "Any relation?"

It was easy to see that the lawyer was used to that. He said: "A cousin."

Guy said: "Let's hope you got the brains. After all, he got the power. It would only be fair."

The famous-name lawyer sat up in his chair and started to say something, but Guy waved his hand like he was holding a magic silencing wand. The lawyer shut up.

I introduced myself. As soon as I did, Guy said, "Not only is Ron a lawyer, he's a liar."

The new patients looked at us with surprise. No one said

anything. Guy didn't look at me, but said: "Isn't that right, Ron?"

I had seen him do this before, so I said: "Sure.'

He waited for me to say something else, which I didn't. The new lawyers were visibly uncomfortable. No one moved. The room was as silent as a courtroom waiting for the jury to deliver its verdict.

After a few minutes, he said: "I don't know the rest of you very well, but I know that Ron is a liar. Lawyer, liar. Isn't it interesting how similar the words are?"

The others looked at me. I smiled and said nothing. I wasn't going to fall for this.

The famous-name lawyer sat up in his chair and said: "Well, if that's your opinion of lawyers, I don't know what I'm doing here or what you're doing here."

Guy smiled and said: "Well, I don't know what you're doing here. I'm here because I was told to be here."

Famous-name said: "Maybe I won't stay here. I thought this was the best place in the world, but I didn't know it was run by assholes."

Guy smiled and said: "Then don't stay here. I don't know anything about you. Maybe you're a liar, too. I don't know. Lawyer, liar. I do know that Ron is a liar." Not looking at me, he again asked "Aren't you, Ron?"

"If you say so."

I looked at him out of the corner of my eye. He was still smiling. He started scratching at some of the spackling on his face.

"You say you are, but I don't get the feeling you mean it."

I said nothing. Another lawyer said: "Wait a second. Is there something going on between the two of you?"

Guy said: "Nope. I hardly know Ron. All I really know is that he's a liar."

Famous-name leaned ever more forward in his chair. "Is this how you treat people here? Insulting their dignity?"

Guy quit picking at his face and loudly laughed. "You're making a classic lawyer mistake. You're assuming that any of you have dignity."

Famous-name turned read and leaned so forward in his chair I thought he'd fall out of it. "I'm not putting up with this!" he shouted.

Guy said: "I can't control what you do."

Famous-name said: "I can! And I can leave if I want!"

Guy said: "You sure can, but then you wouldn't be able to help Ron, and he's such a liar."

I had about had it, too. I was getting very angry.

"Okay, isn't your point made?" I asked.

"The point is for you to admit that you're a liar. Admit it. Just think of what a good lawyer you'd be if you didn't lie."

"I was – am – a good lawyer," I said.

"Yes, but all that's based upon you manipulating people with your charm and wit. Just imagine how good you'd be if you didn't manipulate."

Another lawyer said: "That's the whole point of being a lawyer. We're supposed to manipulate to get people to agree with us."

Famous-name said: "That's what society wants us to do. That's why people hire the baddest, meanest, most manipulative lawyer they can. They only hate us until they're in trouble."

I was thinking that Guy didn't understand the first thing about being a lawyer.

Guy said: "That may be. I don't know about you guys, but I know that Ron would be a great lawyer if he weren't such a liar. Isn't that true, Ron?"

Everything came to a point then for me. I thought I was a great lawyer. But I also realized what he said about manipulation was true. I constantly charmed, argued and manipulated. I did everything to get my own way. I had justified it by saying it was done for a client, but it was really done for my ego. It was really done because I had lived in fear and I needed to feel powerful. I was a liar, especially to myself.

Guy said: "Even Cliff thinks you're a liar."

I got very angry. "Cliff never said that."

"Yes, he did" Guy said. "He just told me before I came in here."

I was very angry, very hot, very fearful and very hurt. Did Cliff really say that? He had never called me a liar. Why would he say that? Was Guy lying?

Guy again said: "Yep. Even Cliff thinks you're a liar."

No one said anything. Famous-name was still on the edge of his chair. He looked ridiculous. He was ready to defend me against what? A name? A concept? Was this about him, Guy, me?

I sat there saying nothing. But I started to smile. I felt a physical sensation as though I was being uncovered. I felt as though there was sunlight shining on me. I felt that warmth and comfort that only lazy, sunny Sunday afternoons gave. I no longer felt like a refugee, an underdog or a soldier fighting an unknown yet vicious enemy.

I looked directly at Guy and said: "I may be a liar, but Cliff loves me."

The other lawyers, especially the new ones, looked at me like I was nuts. What's love got to do with it? A patient being loved by a therapist?

Guy smiled and said: "Yes, Ron. He does love you. Even if you are a liar. He loves you."

I started laughing. "This is one of your set-ups, isn't it? You and Cliff planned this, didn't you?"

"And if we did?"

"Nothing. It's still real. I have been a liar. But I am loved."

I felt so starry eyed. It wasn't a sexual love. It was more than that. It was trust, and comfort and knowing I could lie, disappoint, be good, be bad and still be honestly loved, even with all my pain, my aching obvious wounds, my manipulations and my crimes.

Guy looked at me and said: "You can go now if you want."

I realized he was giving me my discharge. I started to cry a little, but I felt so wonderful. This was what it was all about. Learning to be loved. It sounded so simple, but as I sat there I saw the red faces on the other lawyers, their anger and their anxiety. It was time to leave. I knew it. They needed the group. It was time for me to get ready to rejoin the real world.

I said: "okay."

I got up, smiled, shook his hand and said: "See you later."